Database Management in Practice: Indexing, Backup Strategies, and Optimization

James Relington

DEDICATION

To those who seek knowledge, inspiration, and new perspectives—
may this book be a companion on your journey, a spark for curiosity,
and a reminder that every page turned is a step toward discovery.

AKNOWLEDGEMENTS

I would like to express my deepest gratitude to everyone who contributed to the creation of this book. To my colleagues and mentors, your insights and expertise have been invaluable. A special thank you to my family and friends for their unwavering support and encouragement throughout this journey.

Foundations of Relational Databases

The relational database model is a cornerstone of modern data management systems, shaping the way information is stored, accessed, and manipulated across a wide range of industries. Introduced by Edgar F. Codd in 1970, the relational model revolutionized data storage by proposing that data should be organized in tables, known as relations, with clearly defined relationships between them. Each table, or relation, consists of rows and columns, where rows represent individual records and columns represent attributes of the data. This simple yet powerful structure has allowed relational databases to become the dominant method of data storage in enterprise environments, educational institutions, and government systems.

At the core of relational databases lies the concept of a schema, which defines the structure of data within the system. A schema outlines the tables in the database, the attributes within each table, and the relationships between them. These relationships are typically enforced through the use of keys, specifically primary keys and foreign keys. A primary key uniquely identifies each row in a table, ensuring that no two records are identical. Foreign keys establish a link between tables by referencing the primary key of another table, thereby creating a logical connection that reflects real-world relationships.

One of the most significant advantages of the relational model is its foundation in formal mathematical theory, particularly set theory and predicate logic. This theoretical grounding provides a rigorous and predictable framework for managing data, enabling powerful query capabilities through the use of Structured Query Language, or SQL. SQL allows users to define, manipulate, and retrieve data with a high degree of precision and flexibility. It supports operations such as selection, projection, and join, which can be combined in numerous ways to answer complex business questions.

The concept of data integrity is integral to relational databases. Integrity constraints ensure that the data remains accurate and consistent over time. These constraints include entity integrity, which requires that each table have a unique primary key, and referential integrity, which ensures that foreign keys correctly reference existing primary keys. Additional constraints such as unique, not null, and check can be applied to enforce specific rules on the data, reducing the risk of errors and improving overall data quality.

Another key feature of relational databases is their support for transactions, which are sequences of operations performed as a single logical unit of work. Transactions follow the ACID properties: atomicity, consistency, isolation, and durability. Atomicity guarantees that all operations within a transaction are completed successfully, or none are applied. Consistency ensures that the database transitions from one valid state to another. Isolation maintains the independence of concurrent transactions, preventing conflicts and ensuring data correctness. Durability means that once a transaction is committed, its effects are permanent, even in the event of a system failure.

Normalization is a technique used in relational databases to organize data efficiently and eliminate redundancy. Through a series of normal forms, data is broken down into smaller, related tables, reducing duplication and making the database easier to maintain. Each normal form builds upon the previous one, adding additional rules to ensure that the data structure supports integrity and minimizes anomalies in data operations such as insertions, deletions, and updates. While normalization improves data integrity and reduces storage requirements, it can sometimes lead to complex queries, which is why denormalization is occasionally employed for performance reasons in specific use cases.

Relational databases have been developed and optimized by many vendors, resulting in a wide range of database management systems (DBMS) that implement the relational model. These include popular systems like Oracle Database, Microsoft SQL Server, MySQL, and PostgreSQL. Each of these systems offers various extensions and optimizations, but they all adhere to the fundamental principles of the relational model. The choice of a specific DBMS often depends on the requirements of the application, such as scalability, security, performance, and vendor support.

The reliability and predictability of relational databases make them suitable for transactional systems, where data consistency and accuracy are paramount. Applications such as banking, inventory management, customer relationship management, and enterprise resource planning rely heavily on relational databases to ensure that operations are conducted correctly and efficiently. The ability to model real-world entities and relationships using a structured format allows developers and data analysts to design systems that reflect the needs of the business and provide meaningful insights.

Over the decades, the relational model has proven its resilience and adaptability in the face of evolving technological landscapes. While new data models such as NoSQL and document-oriented databases have emerged to handle specific challenges related to scalability and unstructured data, relational databases remain the preferred choice for a vast array of applications due to their robustness and maturity. Their ability to support complex transactions, enforce integrity constraints, and provide powerful querying capabilities ensures their continued relevance in both traditional and modern computing environments.

Understanding the foundational principles of relational databases is essential for anyone working with data. It provides the conceptual framework necessary for designing effective database schemas, writing efficient queries, and maintaining data integrity. As organizations continue to generate and depend on data for decision-making, the importance of mastering relational database concepts remains undiminished. From simple applications to large-scale enterprise systems, the relational model underpins much of the digital infrastructure that drives today's data-driven world.

Understanding Database Engines

A database engine, often referred to as a storage engine, is the underlying software component that handles the low-level operations of storing, retrieving, and managing data within a database management system. While users typically interact with databases through high-level interfaces like SQL, it is the engine that performs the actual work behind the scenes. Understanding how database engines function is essential for optimizing performance, choosing the right configuration for an application, and diagnosing issues when they arise. Each database engine brings a unique combination of features, limitations, and performance characteristics, and selecting the right one can make a significant difference in both scalability and efficiency.

Database engines are responsible for executing commands sent by the client, such as reading and writing data, enforcing data integrity constraints, maintaining indexes, and ensuring transactional properties. To do this effectively, the engine includes multiple subsystems, including a query processor, transaction manager, buffer manager, and storage manager. The query processor translates high-level queries into low-level instructions that can be executed efficiently. The transaction manager ensures that operations are atomic and follow the rules of ACID. The buffer manager handles caching to minimize disk I/O, while the storage manager interacts with the file system or raw storage to persist data reliably.

There are two primary types of database engines used in relational database systems: row-oriented and column-oriented. Row-oriented engines store data in rows, which is efficient for transactional workloads where entire records are frequently accessed or modified. This format excels in scenarios where data is inserted or updated frequently and when queries retrieve full rows. Column-oriented engines, on the other hand, store data by columns, making them ideal for analytical workloads where queries typically aggregate data from a few columns across many rows. Because only the relevant columns are read during queries, columnar engines significantly reduce the amount of data that must be scanned, which improves performance in read-heavy environments such as data warehousing.

Within a single database system, multiple storage engines might be available, each optimized for different tasks. For example, MySQL supports several storage engines, including InnoDB and MyISAM. InnoDB is the default storage engine in modern versions and supports full ACID compliance, transactions, foreign keys, and row-level locking. It is designed for high reliability and is well-suited for high-concurrency environments. MyISAM, while simpler and faster for read-heavy workloads, lacks many advanced features such as transactions and foreign key constraints. Understanding the differences between these engines is critical when designing systems, as the wrong choice can lead to performance issues or data integrity problems.

Database engines are also responsible for implementing concurrency control mechanisms that manage how multiple users access data simultaneously. Concurrency control ensures that transactions are isolated from one another to prevent problems such as dirty reads, non-repeatable reads, and phantom reads. Most relational database engines use either optimistic or pessimistic concurrency control. Pessimistic control assumes conflicts are likely and locks data preemptively, while optimistic control assumes conflicts are rare and checks for them only when a transaction commits. The approach chosen affects the performance and behavior of concurrent applications and must align with the application's access patterns.

Logging and recovery mechanisms are another vital component of any robust database engine. When a transaction modifies data, the engine records these changes in a transaction log before applying them to the actual database files. This write-ahead logging strategy ensures that in the event of a crash or power failure, the engine can use the log to recover to a consistent state by rolling back incomplete transactions and reapplying committed ones. Recovery procedures are deeply embedded into the architecture of modern engines and contribute significantly to their reliability and trustworthiness in mission-critical environments.

Indexing is handled at the engine level and is central to performance optimization. Depending on the engine's capabilities, it may support a variety of index types, such as B-tree, hash, or full-text indexes. The engine is responsible for maintaining these structures during inserts, updates, and deletes, and using them to accelerate data retrieval during query execution. How indexes are implemented and used by the engine can dramatically impact query performance. Efficient use of indexes, and understanding how the engine evaluates query plans, allows developers and database administrators to optimize their systems intelligently.

Another key element of database engines is memory management. Engines maintain a buffer pool, which caches frequently accessed data in memory to reduce the need for disk I/O. The size and configuration of the buffer pool have a direct impact on performance, particularly in high-throughput systems. Modern engines also support adaptive algorithms to manage memory dynamically based on workload patterns, helping to ensure optimal resource utilization.

Scalability features are increasingly critical as data volumes grow. Some engines are designed for single-node operation, while others support horizontal scaling across multiple nodes, either natively or through third-party tools. For instance, distributed engines like CockroachDB or the engine behind Google Spanner provide horizontal scalability with strong consistency guarantees, making them suitable for global applications. Traditional engines like PostgreSQL have extensions and tools that allow for read replicas and partitioning to manage large datasets, though scaling writes typically requires additional strategies such as sharding.

Understanding the inner workings of database engines provides the foundation for making informed architectural decisions. It enables one to configure the system in a way that aligns with the application's access patterns, ensures high availability, and maintains data integrity under varying workloads. As the complexity of data systems increases, having a solid grasp of how database engines operate becomes not only useful but necessary for anyone involved in database administration, backend development, or data engineering. With this understanding, professionals are better equipped to design systems that are both performant and resilient, capable of meeting the demands of modern applications and users.

Data Types and Storage Considerations

Data types form the structural foundation of any database system, defining the kind of values that can be stored in each column of a table. Choosing the correct data type is not just a matter of syntax or correctness; it has deep implications for performance, storage efficiency, data integrity, and the scalability of a database. Each data type determines how much space is required to store a value, how that value is interpreted by the system, and which operations can be performed on it. Careful planning around data types and their storage considerations is essential in building robust and efficient databases that can serve the needs of modern applications.

When designing a database schema, selecting the smallest appropriate data type for each field helps to reduce the overall size of the data on disk. Smaller data types consume less storage space and allow for more rows to fit in memory or within a single disk page, leading to faster I/O operations and improved cache efficiency. For example, using an integer data type of four bytes to store a value that never exceeds a range suitable for a one-byte tinyint wastes space unnecessarily. When this inefficiency is multiplied across millions of rows, the cumulative impact can be significant in terms of storage and performance.

There are several categories of data types commonly used in relational databases: numeric, character, date and time, binary, and spatial. Numeric types can be broken down further into integers and floating-point numbers. Integer types are generally preferred for keys and counters due to their precision and predictability. Floating-point types, such as float and double, are useful for representing scientific or approximate values, but they may introduce rounding errors and imprecision. Decimal or numeric types, which store exact numbers with fixed precision and scale, are ideal for financial data where accuracy is non-negotiable.

Character data types include fixed-length and variable-length strings. Fixed-length types, such as char, always use the same amount of storage regardless of the length of the actual data, which can lead to unnecessary padding and wasted space. Variable-length types, such as varchar, store only as much space as needed, plus a small overhead to track length. Choosing between char and varchar involves a trade-off between speed and space. Char can be slightly faster in access because of its fixed size, but varchar offers better storage efficiency, especially for fields with highly variable lengths.

Date and time data types are designed to store temporal values, which are vital for tracking when events occur, scheduling operations, and auditing. These data types vary in precision and size, from simple date fields storing only year, month, and day, to timestamp fields capable of recording microsecond or nanosecond precision. The choice depends on the specific needs of the application, as higher precision requires more storage. It is also important to be aware of time zone handling, since storing timestamps without considering time zones can lead to inconsistencies when data is interpreted in different locales.

Binary data types are used to store raw data such as images, documents, or encrypted content. These types are not human-readable and are generally larger in size, making them less suitable for frequent queries or sorting operations. Large binary objects, known as BLOBs, should be used cautiously, as storing large amounts of binary data directly in the database can increase table size dramatically and degrade performance. In many architectures, it is preferable to store such content externally and reference it from the database using a URL or identifier.

Storage engines may handle data types differently, affecting the way data is written to disk and retrieved. Some engines compress data automatically, while others require manual configuration or use plugins to support compression. Data alignment and padding rules can also differ, influencing how efficiently space is used within storage blocks or pages. Understanding the storage model of the underlying engine helps database architects make informed choices about data type selection. Misalignments between intended use and actual storage behavior can lead to fragmentation, wasted space, and degraded performance.

Indexing is also influenced by data types. Shorter and more predictable data types generally result in smaller and more efficient indexes. For example, indexing a fixed-size integer column is faster and more efficient than indexing a long, variable-length text field. In some databases, text fields must be indexed using special full-text indexing mechanisms, which can consume significant resources and require additional maintenance. Choosing appropriate data types with indexing in mind is crucial for ensuring that queries remain performant under heavy load or with large datasets.

Normalization plays a role in managing storage concerns by organizing data in such a way that redundancy is minimized. However, as data becomes more normalized and distributed across multiple tables, joins become more frequent. The cost of these joins can be impacted by data type decisions, especially if columns used in joins are large or inconsistently defined. Ensuring consistent data types between related tables avoids implicit conversions, which can hinder index usage and slow down queries significantly.

In high-performance systems, even the choice between signed and unsigned data types can matter. Unsigned types allow for a greater range of positive values, which is particularly useful in primary key columns or counters that are expected to grow continuously. Being mindful of this detail can delay or prevent the need to upgrade a data type in the future, which would otherwise require a costly migration of all rows in a table.

Ultimately, data types define not just what kind of data can be stored but how that data will behave within the database environment. The implications of data type decisions echo across performance, scalability, indexing, and application behavior. Mastery of data types and their storage considerations is an essential skill for database designers and developers alike, ensuring that systems are not only correct in their logic but also efficient, maintainable, and ready to grow with the needs of the organization.

Normalization and Denormalization

Normalization and denormalization are two fundamental concepts in relational database design that directly impact the structure, efficiency, and performance of a database. These techniques are closely related and often work in tandem, depending on the goals of the database system—whether the priority is data integrity and reduced redundancy, or performance and simplified access patterns. Understanding when and how to apply normalization and denormalization is critical for building robust and efficient databases that meet the functional and operational needs of applications.

Normalization is the process of organizing data in a database to minimize redundancy and dependency. The idea is to divide large, complex tables into smaller, more manageable ones while ensuring that data is stored in only one place. This process results in a set of related tables that are connected through relationships, typically defined by foreign keys. Normalization is guided by a set of rules called normal forms, each of which addresses specific types of redundancy and anomalies. The most commonly used normal forms are the first, second, and third, though higher normal forms exist for more specialized requirements.

In the first normal form, a table must contain only atomic values, meaning each field contains a single, indivisible value. This prevents the use of repeating groups and ensures that each column holds one kind of data. The second normal form builds on the first by requiring that all non-key attributes be fully functionally dependent on the entire primary key, which eliminates partial dependencies in tables with composite keys. The third normal form, one of the most widely applied, requires that all attributes are only dependent on the primary key, thus removing transitive dependencies. Each progression through the normal forms creates a more structured and logically consistent schema, reducing the potential for insert, update, and delete anomalies.

The primary advantage of normalization is data integrity. By ensuring that each piece of information is stored only once, normalized databases reduce the risk of inconsistencies. If a customer's phone number is stored in only one table, then updating it requires a single operation. This not only simplifies maintenance but also enforces a single source of truth. Furthermore, normalized databases make better use of storage by eliminating redundant data, which is particularly valuable in large-scale systems where millions of records are involved. Queries in normalized databases may involve more joins, but the data they return is generally more reliable and accurate.

However, there are scenarios where normalization introduces complexity that can hinder performance. As the data becomes more normalized and distributed across multiple tables, the number of joins required to retrieve commonly used data increases. These joins, especially when executed on large tables with insufficient indexing or inefficient queries, can become performance bottlenecks. This is where denormalization enters the picture as a practical compromise between purity of design and operational efficiency.

Denormalization is the process of intentionally introducing redundancy into a database schema to improve read performance and simplify query structures. By storing duplicate data or precomputed aggregates, denormalized designs reduce the need for expensive joins and enable faster access to frequently needed information. While this approach increases the complexity of data maintenance and the risk of inconsistency, it can offer significant performance benefits in read-heavy environments, such as reporting systems, analytics dashboards, and content management platforms.

One common example of denormalization is storing the total value of an order directly in the orders table, rather than calculating it by summing the values of individual line items each time it is needed. Another example is embedding customer names or product descriptions in transaction records to avoid joining with reference tables for display purposes. These techniques allow for rapid querying and reporting, especially when dealing with large volumes of data and tight response time requirements. However, they come at the cost of increased storage usage and the need for additional logic to keep the duplicated data synchronized when updates occur.

Choosing between normalization and denormalization is not a binary decision, but rather a matter of balance informed by the specific use cases of the application. Online transaction processing systems, which prioritize accuracy and integrity for frequent writes, benefit more from normalized schemas. Conversely, online analytical processing systems, which are optimized for complex queries over large datasets, often require some level of denormalization to achieve acceptable performance. In many real-world applications, both approaches are used within the same system, with core transactional data stored in a normalized format and separate denormalized views or summary tables created for reporting and analysis.

The decision to normalize or denormalize should also consider the anticipated evolution of the data model. Normalized designs tend to be more flexible and easier to modify as new requirements emerge. Adding new attributes or relationships can often be done without significantly altering existing structures. Denormalized systems, on the other hand, may require more extensive changes to accommodate new fields, especially if the same piece of data is repeated across multiple locations.

Ultimately, the effective use of normalization and denormalization reflects a deep understanding of the trade-offs between data integrity, storage efficiency, and performance. Successful database architects and developers know how to apply both principles judiciously, shaping schemas that not only fulfill the logical requirements of the domain but also perform reliably under the workload conditions of the application. Mastery of these concepts enables the creation of systems that are both structurally sound and operationally efficient, capable of scaling gracefully while maintaining the quality and accessibility of the data they manage.

Primary Keys and Foreign Keys

Primary keys and foreign keys are essential constructs in relational database systems, forming the backbone of data integrity and relational structure. They define how data is uniquely identified and how different tables relate to one another. Without primary and foreign keys, relational databases would lose their most fundamental characteristic: the ability to model complex relationships between entities in a consistent and coherent manner. These keys not only enforce rules on data but also make it possible to efficiently navigate and manage large volumes of related information in a scalable way.

A primary key is a column or a combination of columns in a table that uniquely identifies each row in that table. It acts as a unique identifier, ensuring that no two rows can have the same primary key value. This uniqueness is critical for distinguishing records and is a foundational requirement for operations such as updates and deletions, which target specific rows. Every table in a well-designed relational database should have a primary key, because it guarantees the integrity of the data and serves as a stable anchor for relationships with other tables. Primary keys are typically defined on fields that are inherently unique, such as user IDs, product codes, or invoice numbers.

Once a primary key is defined, the database system enforces uniqueness on that column or set of columns automatically. Attempting to insert a duplicate value into a primary key field results in an error, preventing accidental duplication of records. Furthermore, primary keys cannot contain null values, since null represents an unknown or undefined value, and it would contradict the requirement that every row must be uniquely identifiable. This strict rule ensures that each row can always be referenced precisely, which is particularly important when other tables need to establish links to it.

Foreign keys, on the other hand, are used to create and enforce relationships between tables. A foreign key in one table is a column or group of columns that refers to the primary key in another table. This reference establishes a parent-child relationship, where the table containing the foreign key is the child, and the table with the referenced primary key is the parent. Foreign keys ensure referential integrity, which means that a record in the child table must always correspond to an existing record in the parent table. Without this constraint, data inconsistencies could arise, such as orders referring to customers that do not exist.

The enforcement of foreign key constraints helps maintain logical consistency across the database. For example, if a sales order includes a foreign key pointing to a customer ID, that customer must exist in the customers table. If someone tries to insert an order for a non-existent customer, the database will reject the operation. Similarly, if there is an attempt to delete a customer who has associated orders, the database can either block the deletion, cascade the deletion to related rows, or set the foreign key to null, depending on how the foreign key constraint is configured. These behaviors—known as referential actions—allow developers to define how the system should respond to changes in related data.

Primary and foreign keys also play a crucial role in indexing and query optimization. Most database systems automatically create an index on the primary key to speed up access to individual records. Likewise, foreign keys are often indexed, especially if they are used in join operations or queries involving filters. Proper indexing ensures that relationships can be traversed quickly, even in large datasets, and that joins between tables are executed efficiently. Without indexing on key columns, queries can become slow and resource-intensive, especially as the volume of data grows.

In practice, choosing the right columns to serve as primary and foreign keys requires careful thought. Primary keys should be stable, meaning their values should not change frequently. Changing a primary key can have ripple effects, requiring updates to all foreign keys that reference it. Therefore, surrogate keys—system-generated values such as auto-incrementing integers or universally unique identifiers (UUIDs)—are often preferred over natural keys, which are based on real-world data like email addresses or social security numbers. Surrogate keys provide a consistent and opaque way to identify records without embedding business logic into the key itself.

Foreign keys must match the data type and structure of the primary key they reference. This compatibility is necessary for the database engine to enforce referential integrity. When designing a schema, aligning the data types of key columns is essential to prevent runtime errors and ensure that relationships can be established correctly. Moreover, using consistent naming conventions for key columns, such as appending _id to the column name, helps maintain readability and reduces confusion when navigating complex schemas.

While primary and foreign keys introduce valuable structure and safeguards, they also require additional overhead in terms of maintenance and performance. Enforcing these constraints means that every insert, update, or delete operation must be checked against the rules defined by the keys. In systems with extremely high write volumes or in data warehousing scenarios where bulk loads are common, these constraints might be temporarily disabled to speed up operations. However, this practice must be handled with caution, as it opens the door to potential inconsistencies that must be corrected later.

Primary keys and foreign keys are more than technical features; they represent the logical blueprint of the data model. They define how entities are identified and how they relate, ensuring that the database accurately mirrors the business domain it serves. They support integrity, enhance query performance, and enable complex applications to function reliably at scale. Without them, relational databases would lose their defining capability: the ability to represent structured, interrelated data in a way that is both logical and enforceable. As such, understanding and applying these keys correctly is fundamental to the design, operation, and success of any relational database system.

Introduction to Indexing

Indexing is one of the most powerful tools available in a relational database for improving the performance of data retrieval operations. At its core, an index is a data structure that allows the database engine to locate specific rows in a table more quickly, without having to scan every record. This becomes especially important as the volume of data grows, because without indexes, even a simple query could result in a full table scan, consuming significant resources and leading to delays in response times. Proper indexing is a key factor in ensuring that a database remains responsive and scalable under the pressure of increasing user demands and larger datasets.

When a query is executed, the database engine analyzes the requested data and evaluates the most efficient path to retrieve it. Without an index, this path typically involves scanning each row in the table to see if it matches the query conditions. For small tables, this may not be problematic, but as the number of rows increases into the millions or billions, full table scans become prohibitively slow. Indexes mitigate this issue by providing a shortcut—an organized map—that the engine can use to go directly to the rows that match specific criteria. This behavior is comparable to using an index in a book, where instead of reading every page, one can quickly turn to the exact page where a topic is mentioned.

The most common type of index used in relational databases is the B-tree index, short for balanced tree. B-tree indexes maintain their entries in sorted order, which allows the database engine to perform efficient binary searches. This structure makes it ideal for queries involving ranges, equality conditions, and sorting operations. Because B-tree indexes keep their branches balanced, they offer consistent performance regardless of the number of entries, allowing access times to remain logarithmic even as data volume increases. The ability to maintain order also makes B-tree indexes highly useful for ORDER BY and GROUP BY clauses.

Indexes can be created on one or more columns. A single-column index is the simplest form, targeting queries that filter based on one specific attribute. Composite indexes, on the other hand, include multiple columns and are particularly effective for queries that involve conditions on multiple fields. The order of columns in a composite index matters, as it dictates which combinations of columns the index can support efficiently. If a composite index is built on columns A and B, it can accelerate queries filtering by A alone or by A and B together, but not by B alone. Understanding this subtlety is crucial when designing indexes to align with common query patterns.

While indexes greatly enhance read performance, they come with trade-offs that must be carefully considered. One of the most significant is the overhead involved in maintaining indexes during data modification operations. Every time a row is inserted, updated, or deleted, the associated indexes must also be updated to reflect the change. This can lead to performance degradation during write-intensive operations, particularly if too many indexes are defined on a single table. Therefore, it is important to find a balance between the speed of reads and the cost of writes, and to index only those columns that truly benefit from it.

Another consideration is the amount of storage space consumed by indexes. Although they are typically much smaller than the data they index, large tables with multiple indexes can require substantial disk space. Additionally, indexes add to the complexity of the database schema, making maintenance and optimization more challenging over time. When designing indexes, it is essential to focus on the actual usage patterns of the application, favoring those columns most frequently used in WHERE clauses, JOIN conditions, or as part of filtering and sorting.

In addition to the standard B-tree index, many database systems support specialized types of indexes designed for specific use cases. For example, hash indexes provide very fast lookups for equality conditions but are not suitable for range queries or ordering. Full-text indexes are optimized for searching within large bodies of text, supporting functions like stemming and relevance ranking. Spatial indexes are designed for geographical data, allowing efficient querying of spatial relationships like proximity or containment. These specialized indexes extend the capabilities of the database, enabling it to perform well even with complex or domain-specific data.

The creation and management of indexes should be guided by query analysis and performance monitoring. Most modern relational databases include tools such as query execution plans that show how a query was executed and whether an index was used. These insights allow administrators to identify slow-running queries and determine whether the addition or modification of an index could improve performance. It is equally important to periodically review existing indexes, as unused or redundant indexes may be silently degrading performance by increasing the overhead on writes.

Indexing also plays a crucial role in enforcing certain types of constraints. For example, primary key and unique constraints automatically create indexes to ensure that no duplicate values are entered into the specified columns. These indexes not only enforce integrity but can also be used to accelerate queries. Foreign key constraints, while not automatically indexed in all database systems, benefit greatly from indexing to support fast joins between parent and child tables. Failing to index foreign key columns can lead to inefficient query execution plans and unnecessary full table scans.

The effectiveness of indexing is not static, but evolves alongside the application. As data volume increases, as queries change, and as usage patterns shift, previously effective indexes may become less beneficial or even harmful. Ongoing monitoring, benchmarking, and schema tuning are necessary to keep indexes aligned with the performance needs of the system. Indexes should be reviewed as part of regular maintenance routines, especially after significant changes to application logic, data growth, or usage behavior.

Understanding the fundamentals of indexing provides a strong foundation for database optimization. It equips developers and administrators with the knowledge needed to make intelligent decisions that improve response times, reduce resource consumption, and enhance the overall user experience. Indexes are not a silver bullet, but when applied with care and insight, they become an indispensable tool in the ongoing pursuit of performance and scalability in relational database systems.

B-Tree Indexes in Depth

B-tree indexes are the most widely used indexing structure in relational database systems, forming the backbone of efficient data retrieval in a vast array of applications. The B in B-tree stands for balanced, and this characteristic is crucial to its performance. A B-tree is a self-balancing tree structure that maintains sorted data and allows searches, sequential access, insertions, and deletions in logarithmic time. This predictable and consistent performance makes B-tree indexes an ideal choice for general-purpose indexing, supporting both equality lookups and range queries with remarkable efficiency. To fully appreciate the value of B-tree indexes, it is essential to understand how they are structured, how they operate, and how they interact with the database engine during query execution.

At a high level, a B-tree index is composed of a hierarchy of nodes, with a single root node at the top, intermediate nodes forming the internal levels, and leaf nodes at the bottom. Each node contains a number of keys and pointers. In internal nodes, the keys serve as guideposts that direct searches to the appropriate child node, while the pointers reference those children. In the leaf nodes, the keys are accompanied by pointers to the actual table rows, or in some implementations, to the physical location of the data. The balanced nature of the tree ensures that all leaf nodes are at the same depth, meaning that the number of steps required to find any key is always within the same logarithmic range, regardless of where it is located in the index.

When a query is executed that involves a condition on an indexed column, the database engine traverses the B-tree from the root node down to a leaf node, using the keys in each internal node to determine which path to follow. This traversal drastically reduces the number of rows that need to be examined compared to a full table scan. For example, if a table has a million rows and the indexed column is well-distributed, a B-tree index can typically locate the desired record in about 20 steps or fewer. This level of efficiency is what makes B-tree indexes the default choice for most relational databases, particularly for columns used in WHERE clauses, joins, or ORDER BY operations.

One of the most powerful features of B-tree indexes is their ability to support range queries. Because the keys in a B-tree are stored in sorted order, the database engine can easily navigate to the first key that matches the lower bound of a range, and then sequentially scan through the leaf nodes until the upper bound is reached. This is extremely beneficial for queries that retrieve data between two values, such as finding all orders between two dates or all products with prices within a certain range. Without a B-tree index, such queries would require a full scan of the table, examining every row to determine if it falls within the specified range.

B-tree indexes also play a critical role in sorting and grouping operations. Since the keys are stored in a sorted manner, queries that require data to be sorted on an indexed column can avoid an expensive sort operation by simply reading the data in order from the index. This is particularly useful in pagination queries and reporting applications, where results need to be displayed in a specific order. Additionally, aggregate functions like MIN and MAX can be optimized using B-tree indexes, as the smallest and largest values are located at the beginning and end of the leaf level, respectively.

In addition to single-column indexes, B-trees can be used to create composite indexes that span multiple columns. The structure of a composite B-tree index follows the same principles, but with keys composed of concatenated column values. These indexes are most effective when queries use the leading column or combination of columns in the same order as defined in the index. If a composite index is built on columns A, B, and C, then queries filtering by A alone or by A and B together can fully benefit from the index. However, if the query skips the leading column and filters only on B or C, the index may not be used efficiently, or at all. Therefore, understanding the order of columns in a composite index is essential for maximizing its utility.

Maintenance of B-tree indexes is another important aspect to consider. Because the structure must remain balanced, insertions and deletions can trigger reorganization of the tree. When a new key is added, the engine finds the appropriate leaf node, inserts the key, and if the node exceeds its capacity, it is split, and a portion of its keys are moved to a new node. This split may propagate upward if necessary, but due to the logarithmic nature of the structure, such events are infrequent and generally do not degrade performance. Deletions may cause nodes to underflow, prompting a merge with a neighboring node or a redistribution of keys, again preserving the balance of the tree.

Although B-tree indexes are highly efficient, they are not without overhead. Every index consumes storage space, and the more indexes a table has, the more time the database must spend maintaining them during insert, update, or delete operations. This overhead can become significant in write-heavy workloads, where the cost of maintaining the index structure can outweigh the benefits of fast reads. Consequently, it is important to evaluate the trade-offs of each index and to avoid unnecessary duplication or indexing of low-selectivity columns that do not filter out a significant portion of rows.

Database administrators and developers must also be mindful of fragmentation within B-tree indexes. Over time, especially with frequent updates and deletes, the index pages can become fragmented, leading to suboptimal performance. Many databases provide tools to monitor and defragment indexes, either manually or through automated maintenance tasks. Rebuilding or reorganizing an index can help restore its original structure and improve query performance by reducing the number of page reads required during traversal.

The prevalence of B-tree indexes in relational databases speaks to their versatility and effectiveness. They are capable of supporting a wide range of query patterns, from simple lookups to complex range scans, and they do so with a high degree of efficiency. A deep understanding of how B-tree indexes function allows database professionals to design schemas that perform well under diverse workloads, ensuring that data remains accessible and operations remain fast as systems grow in complexity and scale.

Hash Indexes and Their Use Cases

Hash indexes are a specialized form of indexing used in database systems to facilitate extremely fast data retrieval for equality comparisons. Unlike B-tree indexes, which maintain their data in a sorted structure and support both equality and range queries, hash indexes focus solely on exact-match searches. Their internal organization relies on a hashing function, which transforms a key into a fixed-size value, known as a hash code, that determines the location of the associated data. This method provides near-constant time complexity for lookups, which can be advantageous in scenarios where performance is critical and queries are highly repetitive or predictable.

The core mechanism of a hash index involves applying a hash function to the value being indexed. This hash function generates a numeric hash value, which the index uses to determine the bucket or slot where the actual data pointer is stored. When a query is issued to find a specific value, the database applies the same hash function to the input, then quickly navigates to the corresponding bucket to retrieve the associated row. Because the hash function distributes values uniformly across a range of buckets, this approach ensures a minimal number of comparisons and avoids the need to traverse a hierarchical tree structure like in B-tree indexes.

Hash indexes excel in scenarios where queries involve equality conditions on highly selective columns. A common example would be looking up a user by their exact user ID or fetching a record by a unique identifier such as a product SKU or transaction number. In these cases, hash indexes can outperform B-tree indexes because they eliminate the need to navigate through ordered nodes and instead allow the system to jump directly to the relevant location. This performance gain becomes especially noticeable in systems that perform a high volume of such queries under strict latency requirements.

Despite their speed in exact matches, hash indexes have notable limitations. One of the most significant is their inability to support range queries. Since the hash function scrambles the natural order of values, there is no logical sequence in the buckets that would allow for comparison operations such as greater than, less than, or between. This makes hash indexes unsuitable for any queries that require scanning through a range of values or sorting results based on the indexed field. Consequently, they are not helpful for clauses that involve ORDER BY or range-based filtering.

Another limitation of hash indexes is the possibility of collisions. A collision occurs when two distinct input values are hashed to the same bucket. When this happens, the database must store both entries in a way that preserves their uniqueness and enables correct retrieval, typically through chaining or open addressing. While modern hashing algorithms are designed to minimize collisions, they cannot eliminate them entirely. A high rate of collisions can degrade performance, as the system must search within a bucket to find the correct entry, which increases the time complexity and may offset the intended efficiency.

The usefulness of hash indexes also depends heavily on the quality of the hash function. A poorly designed hash function that does not distribute values evenly across buckets can lead to clustering, where a disproportionate number of entries fall into a small number of buckets. This phenomenon increases the average lookup time and reduces the advantage of using a hash index in the first place. Therefore, implementing or selecting a robust, well-distributed hash function is crucial for maintaining performance consistency.

In terms of practical use cases, hash indexes are often implemented in systems where key-based lookups dominate and where rapid access is more important than versatility. Key-value stores and in-memory databases such as Redis and Memcached use hash-based structures extensively to ensure microsecond-level response times. In relational databases, hash indexes are more selectively used and may be available only under certain configurations or storage engines. For example, MySQL's MEMORY storage engine uses hash indexes by default for its in-memory tables, optimizing for performance when dealing with ephemeral data that requires fast, repeated access.

Hash indexes also play a vital role in hash joins and hash aggregations during query execution. In these operations, the database engine creates an in-memory hash table to match rows from one table with corresponding rows from another. This temporary index enables fast lookup and combination of data, significantly improving the performance of join operations, particularly when one of the tables is small enough to fit entirely in memory. Although these hash structures are not persistent like traditional indexes, they rely on the same principles and demonstrate the power of hashing in relational operations.

Another area where hash indexes are beneficial is in partitioned tables. When a table is partitioned based on a hash of one or more columns, the data is distributed across multiple physical or logical segments. This approach helps with parallel processing and reduces contention in high-concurrency environments. The hash function determines which partition a row belongs to, allowing the database to target specific partitions when executing queries, thereby improving efficiency and scalability. Hash partitioning is especially useful in distributed databases, where data locality and load balancing are essential concerns.

Security is another dimension where hashing intersects with indexing, though not in the traditional sense. While hash indexes are not designed for cryptographic purposes, the idea of hashing data for comparison plays a role in indexing encrypted or anonymized values. For example, some systems hash personally identifiable information like email addresses or phone numbers to create an index that supports lookups without exposing the original data. This technique allows organizations to maintain a balance between performance and privacy, especially in contexts governed by data protection regulations.

Choosing to use a hash index requires a clear understanding of the workload and query patterns of the application. When the requirements align—specifically, frequent equality-based searches on unique or highly selective fields—hash indexes can offer unmatched performance benefits. However, due to their limitations, they should not be used indiscriminately. Developers and database administrators must analyze the structure of their data and the nature of their queries before implementing hash indexes as part of their indexing strategy.

Understanding hash indexes and their use cases equips database professionals with a valuable optimization tool that, when applied appropriately, can significantly enhance the performance of read-heavy systems. While not a universal solution, hash indexes offer speed and efficiency for specific scenarios, making them an essential component in the broader landscape of indexing techniques in relational databases.

Bitmap Indexes for Analytical Workloads

Bitmap indexes are a powerful indexing mechanism particularly suited for analytical workloads where complex queries must be executed over large volumes of data. Unlike traditional indexing structures such as B-trees or hash indexes, bitmap indexes use bitmaps, which are arrays of bits, to represent the presence or absence of a value in a column for each row in the table. This unique structure allows for incredibly fast set-based operations, making bitmap indexes especially effective in environments such as data warehouses, business intelligence platforms, and online analytical processing systems. These environments are characterized by infrequent updates but frequent and often complex read operations involving aggregations, filtering, and joins.

In a bitmap index, each distinct value in a column is represented by a separate bitmap. Each bit in the bitmap corresponds to a row in the table. If a particular row contains the value that the bitmap represents, the bit for that row is set to one; otherwise, it is set to zero. For example, in a column representing a gender field with values like Male and Female, two bitmaps are created, one for each value. The advantage of this representation becomes clear when queries involve filtering, combining, or analyzing multiple attributes at once. Logical bitwise operations such as AND, OR, and NOT can be applied directly to the bitmaps to efficiently determine the set of rows that meet specific criteria.

Bitmap indexes are extremely space-efficient when used on low-cardinality columns—columns that have a small number of distinct values. These include fields such as gender, marital status, country code, and yes/no flags. Because each value is represented by a single bitmap and the bits can be compressed using efficient run-length encoding techniques, the overall storage footprint of bitmap indexes is often much smaller than that of traditional indexes. This compression not only saves disk space but also improves performance by reducing the amount of data that must be scanned during query execution.

The true strength of bitmap indexes emerges when they are used in combination across multiple low-cardinality columns. Analytical queries often involve filters on several attributes at once, such as finding all customers who are married, live in a certain region, and have subscribed to a newsletter. Instead of scanning the table or even traversing multiple B-tree indexes, the database engine can simply retrieve the relevant bitmaps for each condition and apply logical operations to produce the final result. Because bitwise operations are computationally inexpensive and can be parallelized, the response times for such queries are significantly reduced, even when dealing with millions of rows.

Another advantage of bitmap indexes is their ability to handle ad hoc queries effectively. In many analytical systems, users perform unpredictable queries that combine different columns in various ways to explore trends, identify patterns, or generate reports. Bitmap indexes are not limited by the order of columns, as composite B-tree indexes are. This means that bitmap indexes can support a wide variety of filter combinations without the need to define a large number of multi-column indexes. This flexibility simplifies index management and improves the user experience in exploratory analytical environments.

Despite their strengths, bitmap indexes are not suited for all types of workloads. One major limitation is their performance in write-heavy environments. Every time a row is inserted, updated, or deleted, the corresponding bitmaps must be updated as well. Since each bitmap potentially spans the entire table, modifying even a single row may require rewriting large portions of the bitmap data. This makes bitmap indexes less ideal for transactional systems or applications where data is frequently modified. In such environments, the overhead of maintaining bitmap indexes can outweigh the benefits they offer during query execution.

To mitigate this, many systems implement hybrid strategies. For example, bitmap indexes may be built on materialized views or summary tables that are periodically refreshed rather than on the main transactional tables. This allows the system to benefit from fast analytical queries while isolating the performance cost of maintaining the bitmaps to specific maintenance windows. Some modern database engines also implement adaptive indexing strategies, selectively using bitmap indexes based on data volatility and access patterns.

Bitmap indexes also play a role in improving join performance in analytical workloads. In data warehousing scenarios, star schemas and snowflake schemas are common, with a central fact table and multiple dimension tables. When performing joins between the fact table and dimension tables, bitmap indexes on foreign key columns can significantly speed up the process. By filtering the dimension table using its attributes and then applying bitmap filtering to the corresponding foreign key in the fact table, the database can avoid unnecessary scanning and reduce the computational cost of the join.

Another area where bitmap indexes shine is in query optimization involving aggregation. Bitmap indexes can be used to quickly identify relevant rows for aggregation functions like COUNT, SUM, and AVG. Since bitmaps can represent large sets of rows in a compact form, the database engine can perform preliminary filtering and counting operations before accessing the actual data. This layered approach speeds up query execution and improves overall throughput in systems where responsiveness is critical.

Bitmap indexes are also highly effective when combined with parallel processing techniques. Because bitmaps are simple arrays of bits, they can be split and processed across multiple CPU cores or nodes in a distributed database system. Each processor can perform bitmap operations on its partition of data independently, and the results can be merged efficiently. This parallelism contributes to the scalability of bitmap-based indexing systems, allowing them to handle ever-growing datasets without a linear increase in query times.

Understanding the internal mechanics and ideal use cases of bitmap indexes provides database designers and administrators with a potent tool for optimizing analytical workloads. When used correctly, bitmap indexes can transform the performance of read-intensive systems, enabling fast, responsive, and flexible data exploration even as the volume of data scales into the billions of rows. However, the key to effective use lies in aligning the characteristics of the index with the nature of the workload. With thoughtful implementation, bitmap indexes can unlock the full potential of modern analytical databases, providing the speed and efficiency required to meet today's demanding data analysis needs.

Full-Text Indexing Techniques

Full-text indexing is a specialized technique in database systems designed to handle and optimize the searching of large volumes of textual data. Unlike traditional indexing methods such as B-tree or hash indexes that are effective for exact matches or range queries on structured data, full-text indexing is tailored for unstructured or semi-structured text, enabling efficient and intelligent retrieval of documents or text-based fields that contain specific words or phrases. This type of indexing is critical in applications where the ability to search through narratives, descriptions, logs, articles, or emails plays a central role. Use cases for full-text indexing range from content management systems and knowledge bases to e-commerce search engines and social media platforms.

At the core of full-text indexing lies the process of tokenization, which involves breaking a block of text into individual units called tokens, usually words. During the indexing phase, the system scans each piece of text, identifies tokens, and builds an inverted index, which is essentially a mapping from each unique word to the list of documents or rows in which that word appears. This structure is highly optimized for quick lookup, allowing queries like find all articles containing the word performance or all reviews mentioning excellent and service to be executed efficiently. The inverted index can also store the positions of words within documents, enabling proximity and phrase searches.

Normalization plays a critical role in making full-text indexing effective. This includes processes such as lowercasing all words to ensure case insensitivity, removing common punctuation, and optionally performing stemming and lemmatization. Stemming reduces words to their root form, so that words like running, ran, and runs are indexed as run. Lemmatization goes a step further by applying linguistic rules to map inflected forms to a common base. These normalization techniques expand the power of full-text searches by allowing queries to match semantically similar words and variations, improving recall without significantly compromising precision.

Another important component of full-text indexing is stop word filtering. Stop words are commonly used words such as and, the, or, and is that appear frequently in nearly all texts but typically carry little semantic weight. Including them in the index would increase storage and processing overhead without improving search quality. Therefore, most full-text indexing engines maintain a list of stop words that are ignored during both indexing and querying. Customizing the stop word list can be necessary in certain domains where commonly ignored words may carry special meaning, such as in legal or medical texts.

Ranking and scoring are also central to full-text indexing, especially when results need to be ordered by relevance. Most systems implement scoring algorithms based on term frequency and inverse document frequency, commonly known as TF-IDF. Term frequency reflects how often a word appears in a document, under the assumption that more frequent words are more indicative of the document's subject. Inverse document frequency reduces the weight of words that appear in many documents, since such words are less effective at distinguishing relevant content. By combining these metrics, the system can prioritize documents that mention the search term frequently but not universally.

Boolean search capabilities enhance the flexibility of full-text queries by allowing logical combinations of terms. Operators such as AND, OR, and NOT let users construct complex conditions to narrow or broaden the scope of a search. Phrase search capabilities add another layer of depth by supporting queries that require exact sequences of words, such as customer satisfaction rating. This is made possible by the positional data stored in the inverted index, which enables the engine to verify the order and adjacency of tokens in the original text.

Proximity searches allow users to find documents where words occur within a certain distance from each other. This is especially useful in identifying documents where a contextual relationship exists between terms, such as payment within five words of failure. Proximity queries rely heavily on the storage of word positions and often require more memory and processing power, but they significantly enhance the expressiveness and usefulness of search functionality in domains where the relationship between terms matters more than their mere presence.

Many full-text indexing systems also support language-specific configurations. Tokenization, stemming, and stop words vary significantly across languages. A full-text search engine designed for English might perform poorly on German or Arabic unless it is properly configured. Advanced systems allow per-column or per-table language settings so that multilingual datasets can be indexed and queried accurately. This capability is particularly important for global applications that serve users across multiple linguistic regions and need to deliver relevant results in diverse contexts.

Security and access control considerations must also be integrated into full-text indexing strategies. In multi-user environments, search results must be filtered based on user permissions, ensuring that users cannot retrieve or infer the existence of documents they are not authorized to see. Implementing security-aware indexing often involves combining the full-text index with metadata filters or access control lists at query time, which can introduce complexity but is essential for maintaining data confidentiality and integrity.

The implementation of full-text indexes can vary significantly across different database engines and platforms. Relational database systems like MySQL and PostgreSQL offer native full-text indexing features, but often come with limitations in terms of ranking algorithms, language support, or scalability. To overcome these constraints, many developers integrate dedicated full-text search engines like Elasticsearch, Apache Solr, or Sphinx, which offer more advanced indexing and querying capabilities. These systems are designed from the ground up to support full-text workloads, providing better performance, richer query syntax, and more control over index configuration.

Maintenance of full-text indexes requires attention, especially in systems with frequent data changes. When new documents are added or existing ones are modified, the index must be updated accordingly to reflect the current content. Some systems support real-time or near-real-time indexing, ensuring that new content becomes searchable with minimal delay. Others use batch processes to periodically rebuild or refresh the index. Understanding the update model of the indexing system is crucial for maintaining both the freshness of results and overall system performance.

Full-text indexing techniques offer unmatched capabilities when it comes to searching large collections of unstructured text. Their ability to handle linguistic complexity, support expressive queries, and deliver relevant results quickly makes them indispensable in modern information systems. As the volume of textual data continues to grow, the importance of efficient, accurate, and scalable full-text indexing will only increase, making it a critical area of expertise for database architects and application developers alike.

Composite and Covering Indexes

Composite and covering indexes are advanced indexing strategies in relational database systems that significantly enhance the performance of queries involving multiple columns. While a single-column index can improve search speed for queries filtered on just one field, real-world applications often involve conditions on several columns simultaneously. Composite indexes, which include two or more columns in a single index structure, are designed to address these more complex query requirements. Covering indexes take the concept a step further by including all the columns needed to satisfy a query, not just those in the WHERE clause, allowing the database engine to answer the query using only the index itself without accessing the underlying table.

A composite index is an ordered structure that allows efficient retrieval of data when queries filter or sort based on a combination of columns. The order of columns in a composite index is critical because it determines which queries can make use of the index efficiently. For example, if a composite index is created on the columns (last_name, first_name), then it will be effective for queries filtering on last_name alone, or on both last_name and first_name together. However, it will not be as effective for queries that filter only on first_name, since the index is structured to optimize access paths beginning with last_name. This prefix rule is one of the most important principles to understand when designing composite indexes. The index can be used as long as the leading column or columns in the query match the leading columns of the index definition.

Composite indexes are extremely useful in scenarios where queries consistently target the same combination of fields. For example, in an e-commerce application, users might frequently search for products by category and price. Creating a composite index on (category, price) allows such queries to be resolved quickly. Additionally, composite indexes are helpful for sorting operations. If the ORDER BY clause in a query matches the column order in a composite index, the database can return sorted results directly from the index, avoiding an expensive sort step during execution.

Covering indexes build upon composite indexes by including all the columns that a query needs, whether for filtering, joining, grouping, or selecting. This means that the index contains not only the key columns used to find the rows but also the additional columns required to fulfill the query output. When a covering index is used, the database engine can retrieve the requested information directly from the index without having to perform a lookup in the base table. This dramatically improves performance, especially for read-heavy systems, by reducing I/O operations and speeding up access.

To illustrate, consider a query that retrieves customer names and email addresses where the status is 'active'. If there is an index on (status, name, email), and these columns are all that the query needs, then the database can satisfy the query entirely from the index. This is particularly powerful in systems with large tables, where accessing the table itself can be costly in terms of disk operations or memory usage. Covering indexes are especially beneficial when the table contains wide rows with many columns but most queries only use a small subset of them.

One of the key design considerations with composite and covering indexes is the trade-off between read efficiency and write overhead. While these indexes can significantly accelerate query performance, they do introduce additional cost when data is inserted, updated, or deleted. Every change to the underlying table must be reflected in the index, and the more columns the index includes, the greater the maintenance overhead. This is particularly relevant in systems with high write activity, where the time spent updating indexes can become a bottleneck. Therefore, it is important to analyze query patterns and apply these indexing strategies only where the performance gain justifies the additional cost.

Another important aspect of composite and covering indexes is their size. Including multiple columns or large data types in an index can increase its storage footprint significantly. This can lead to increased memory usage for cached indexes and may impact the performance of other parts of the system. Compression techniques and index-only strategies can mitigate some of these issues, but careful planning is essential to balance storage and performance. For columns with large text or binary data, it is generally not advisable to include them in covering indexes unless absolutely necessary, due to the substantial impact on index size.

In many database systems, covering indexes can be created implicitly using the INCLUDE clause, which allows non-key columns to be added to the index. These additional columns are not part of the sorting structure but are stored in the index leaf nodes. This allows the index to cover more queries without affecting the order of the index or the prefix rules that govern composite key usage. For example, a covering index might be defined as (user_id) INCLUDE (email, last_login), allowing queries that filter by user_id and return email and last_login to be resolved entirely using the index.

Understanding how the query planner interacts with composite and covering indexes is crucial for effective tuning. Execution plans can show whether an index is being used, whether the access is a seek or a scan, and whether the index alone is sufficient to satisfy the query. Monitoring these plans helps in identifying which indexes are providing value and which are not being utilized. It also assists in making informed decisions about which indexes to create, modify, or drop. Keeping the index strategy aligned with real usage patterns ensures optimal performance and prevents unnecessary resource consumption.

As data volumes continue to grow and applications become more complex, the need for intelligent indexing strategies becomes more pressing. Composite and covering indexes offer powerful ways to tailor indexing to the actual behavior of the application. When used judiciously, they can eliminate performance bottlenecks, accelerate user-facing operations, and reduce the load on database resources. However, their design requires a deep understanding of query execution, data distribution, and workload characteristics. Database administrators and developers must continuously evaluate and refine their index strategies to adapt to changing requirements and evolving data landscapes.

Mastering composite and covering indexes provides a vital advantage in building scalable and responsive database systems. These tools enable the efficient execution of complex queries that span multiple conditions and return specific subsets of data. By minimizing the need to access the full table and by reducing the number of logical reads required to process a query, these indexes form a critical part of the database performance optimization toolkit. With proper implementation and ongoing analysis, they help ensure that even under the stress of heavy workloads, the system remains fast, efficient, and capable of delivering a seamless experience to users.

Index Maintenance and Rebuilding

Index maintenance and rebuilding are critical aspects of managing relational database systems that aim to ensure continued query performance, data integrity, and system stability. Over time, as data is inserted, updated, and deleted, the underlying structures of indexes can become fragmented, bloated, or misaligned with the current data distribution. These changes degrade the efficiency of index-based operations, leading to slower queries and increased resource consumption. A proactive and well-planned approach to index maintenance is essential for keeping the database responsive and scalable, especially in high-volume or mission-critical environments where performance bottlenecks can impact application availability and user experience.

Indexes are dynamic structures. Every time a row is inserted into a table, the database engine must also insert a corresponding entry into each associated index. Similarly, when a row is deleted or updated, the index must reflect these changes. Over time, particularly in systems with frequent writes, this constant flux can lead to fragmentation within the index pages. Fragmentation occurs when the logical ordering of index entries no longer matches their physical placement on disk. This results in more page reads during index scans, increased I/O latency, and less efficient use of storage and memory caches. In heavily fragmented indexes, what should be a fast seek operation becomes a series of scattered reads, ultimately harming performance.

To combat fragmentation and other issues, databases support index maintenance operations such as reorganizing and rebuilding indexes. Reorganizing an index is a lighter operation that defragments the leaf level of the index by reordering the entries without fully recreating the structure. It is less resource-intensive and can often be performed online, meaning it does not block access to the table. Rebuilding an index, on the other hand, is a more thorough process. It drops the existing index and recreates it from scratch, rebuilding the structure in a more compact and efficient form. This operation can resolve not only fragmentation but also reduce the size of the index and update statistics, leading to more accurate query optimization decisions.

Deciding whether to reorganize or rebuild an index depends on the degree of fragmentation and the specific capabilities of the database engine. Many systems provide guidelines, such as reorganizing when fragmentation is moderate and rebuilding when it is severe. Fragmentation levels can be monitored through dynamic management views or system catalogs, which report metrics such as average page density, logical fragmentation percentage, and page count. Regularly analyzing these metrics helps administrators determine which indexes require attention and prioritize maintenance tasks based on impact and resource availability.

Index maintenance is not limited to dealing with fragmentation. Statistics associated with indexes must also be kept up to date. These statistics inform the query optimizer about the distribution of values in a column, allowing it to choose the most efficient execution plan. As data changes, these statistics become stale, leading the optimizer to make suboptimal decisions. Some databases update statistics automatically, while others require manual intervention or configuration of update thresholds. Incorporating statistics updates into index maintenance routines ensures that the optimizer continues to make informed choices, which directly affects query performance.

Scheduling index maintenance requires careful consideration of workload patterns and system availability. Performing a rebuild operation on a large index can be resource-intensive, consuming CPU, memory, and I/O bandwidth. On busy systems, such operations may cause contention with user queries or background processes. As a result, maintenance is often scheduled during low-traffic periods, such as overnight or on weekends. Some databases support online index rebuilding, allowing the index to be rebuilt without locking the underlying table. However, this feature may come with trade-offs in terms of resource usage or support for certain types of indexes.

Automation is an essential tool in managing index maintenance at scale. Modern database systems and management tools support job scheduling, monitoring, and alerting, allowing administrators to define maintenance plans that run at regular intervals. These plans can include thresholds for fragmentation, scripts for reorganizing or rebuilding indexes, and logging mechanisms to track progress and outcomes. In environments with hundreds or thousands of indexes, automation ensures consistency, reduces human error, and frees up valuable time for higher-level optimization tasks.

Over-indexing is another challenge that can arise without regular review and maintenance. As applications evolve, new indexes are added to support emerging queries or features, but old indexes may remain even when they are no longer needed. These unused indexes consume disk space, slow down write operations, and increase the complexity of maintenance routines. Part of responsible index maintenance involves periodically reviewing index usage statistics to identify which indexes are actively used by queries and which are candidates for removal. Dropping unnecessary indexes simplifies the schema and improves overall system performance.

Special consideration must also be given to partitioned tables and indexes. In large-scale systems, data is often partitioned by time or category to improve manageability and performance. Indexes on partitioned tables can be either global or local, with each type having different maintenance characteristics. Local indexes are tied to individual partitions and can be rebuilt independently, which is useful for minimizing the scope of maintenance operations. Global indexes span the entire table and may require full rebuilding when partitions are dropped or merged. Understanding these nuances helps database professionals maintain optimal performance in partitioned environments without disrupting ongoing operations.

Security and compliance also intersect with index maintenance. In regulated environments, maintenance operations may need to be logged, audited, or approved through change management processes. Indexes themselves may include sensitive data, especially in covering indexes that store non-key columns. Maintenance procedures must respect access controls and ensure that data handling complies with organizational policies and external regulations. Including security considerations in the maintenance plan helps avoid unintended exposure of data and supports broader governance objectives.

In summary, index maintenance and rebuilding are not one-time tasks but ongoing responsibilities that require regular attention, strategic planning, and technical insight. They involve more than just reacting to performance degradation—they are proactive measures that keep a database agile, efficient, and ready to meet the demands of changing applications. A well-maintained set of indexes contributes not only to faster query execution but also to better use of resources, more accurate query plans, and a healthier overall database environment. The continuous monitoring, analysis, and adjustment of indexes ensure that the database infrastructure remains a strong foundation for reliable and performant data-driven systems.

Measuring Index Efficiency

Measuring index efficiency is a critical aspect of database performance tuning and optimization. While indexes are designed to accelerate data access and reduce query response times, not all indexes deliver the same value, and some may even hinder performance if they are poorly designed or no longer relevant. As data evolves and query patterns shift, indexes that were once beneficial can become burdensome, consuming resources without providing a proportional return. Therefore, continuously evaluating index efficiency is essential to maintaining a responsive, scalable, and cost-effective database system.

The first step in measuring index efficiency involves understanding how often each index is being used. Most modern database management systems provide tools or dynamic views that track index usage statistics, such as the number of times an index has been accessed during query execution. These metrics can reveal which indexes are heavily relied upon and which are seldom or never used. For example, if an index has not been accessed in a significant amount of time, it may be a candidate for removal. However, these metrics must be interpreted with caution, especially in systems that are restarted frequently or in environments where statistics are reset periodically. It is important to consider usage over a representative timeframe that reflects typical workloads.

Another key metric for evaluating index efficiency is the ratio of seeks to scans. An index seek indicates that the database engine was able to use the index to jump directly to the relevant rows, which is a highly efficient operation. An index scan, on the other hand, means that the engine had to examine all or most of the entries in the index to find the required data, which is significantly less efficient. High numbers of scans relative to seeks may suggest that the index is not selective enough or that it is not well aligned with the query's filtering criteria. This often occurs when an index is built on a column with low cardinality or when the index does not match the leading column in a multi-column filter.

Index selectivity is a vital concept in this context. Selectivity refers to how well an index distinguishes between rows in a table. A highly selective index, such as one on a unique identifier or a column with many distinct values, can dramatically reduce the number of rows that need to be examined during a query. Conversely, indexes on columns with few unique values, like a status flag or a gender field, may not provide much benefit for filtering operations. Measuring selectivity involves comparing the number of unique values in the indexed column to the total number of rows in the table. This information can often be found in the database's statistics or system catalogs.

Query execution plans provide a more detailed and context-specific way to measure index efficiency. Execution plans show how the database engine intends to execute a query, including which indexes will be used, how they will be used, and what operations will be performed. By analyzing execution plans, database administrators can determine whether an index is being used optimally or if the engine is choosing to ignore it in favor of a table scan. Reasons for an index being bypassed may include outdated statistics, query predicates that do not match the index structure, or a better-performing competing index. Regularly reviewing execution plans for frequently run or high-impact queries is a practical method for validating index effectiveness.

Another dimension to consider is the maintenance cost associated with each index. Every index adds overhead during insert, update, and delete operations, because the database must ensure that all indexes remain consistent with the underlying table. This means that even unused or underutilized indexes can degrade performance indirectly by increasing the time and resources needed for data modification. Measuring index maintenance costs involves tracking how often an index is updated relative to how often it is read. If an index is frequently maintained but rarely used, its presence may be doing more harm than good.

Storage footprint is also a factor in index efficiency. Indexes consume disk space, and some, particularly those with wide key columns or many included columns, can be quite large. Excessive index size can lead to increased I/O during queries and can strain memory resources when indexes are loaded into cache. Monitoring index size in relation to the benefits they provide helps maintain a lean and efficient indexing strategy. Some database systems allow administrators to monitor the fragmentation level of indexes as well, which affects performance and can be another sign that an index is not operating efficiently.

Measuring the performance impact of index changes through testing is an effective way to validate assumptions about index efficiency. This often involves creating or dropping indexes in a test environment and running representative workloads to compare performance metrics. Benchmarking tools can help quantify the impact of index adjustments on query execution time, CPU usage, memory consumption, and I/O activity. These empirical results provide the most reliable basis for deciding whether to keep, modify, or remove an index.

It is also important to assess how indexes interact with one another. In some cases, multiple indexes may overlap in function, leading to redundancy. For instance, a table may have one index on column A and another on columns A and B. If the latter index is always used in queries that involve both columns, the first index may be unnecessary. Identifying such overlaps requires careful analysis of query patterns and index coverage. Tools and scripts that analyze index overlap can assist in identifying opportunities to consolidate or streamline indexes without sacrificing performance.

Ultimately, measuring index efficiency is not a one-time task but an ongoing process. It requires continuous monitoring, analysis, and adjustment as the application and its data grow and change. Effective index management relies on a deep understanding of the workload, the data model, and the behavior of the query optimizer. By regularly evaluating which indexes are contributing to performance and which are not, database professionals can ensure that indexing strategies remain aligned with system objectives and that resources are used effectively. An efficient set of indexes translates into faster queries, more stable performance, and a more maintainable database infrastructure.

Database Statistics and Query Plans

Database statistics and query plans are fundamental components of query optimization in relational database management systems. These two elements work together behind the scenes to determine the most efficient way for the database engine to execute SQL statements. Understanding how they operate and influence performance is crucial for developers, database administrators, and system architects who aim to build high-performing, scalable applications. While users often focus on writing correct SQL, the way that SQL is interpreted and executed by the engine can vary dramatically depending on the statistics the database has collected and the decisions made in the query plan.

Database statistics are metadata that describe the distribution and characteristics of data within tables and indexes. They include information such as the number of rows in a table, the number of distinct values in a column, the frequency of specific values, data distribution histograms, and the density of values in composite indexes. This statistical data is collected by the database engine through sampling or full scans, depending on the configuration, and is used by the query optimizer to make educated guesses about how to execute a query most efficiently. Without accurate statistics, the optimizer might choose a suboptimal execution path, leading to slow query performance, excessive memory usage, or high disk I/O.

The process of gathering statistics is known as statistics collection or analysis, and it can be triggered manually or automatically. Many modern relational databases include features that automatically update statistics when a certain percentage of the data changes, ensuring that the optimizer always has up-to-date information. However, this automatic updating may not occur frequently enough in some cases, especially in systems with rapid or irregular data changes. For this reason, administrators sometimes configure manual jobs to analyze tables and indexes at regular intervals. Ensuring the freshness of statistics is a key aspect of performance tuning and should be part of routine database maintenance.

Once statistics are collected, they become essential inputs to the query optimizer, the component responsible for generating the query plan. The query optimizer evaluates multiple strategies for retrieving the requested data and selects the one with the lowest estimated cost. This cost is not measured in terms of time but in abstract units based on estimated CPU usage, I/O operations, memory consumption, and other resource considerations. The quality of the optimizer's decisions is directly tied to the accuracy and granularity of the available statistics. If the statistics underestimate or overestimate the size of result sets or the selectivity of predicates, the optimizer might choose a plan that performs poorly in practice.

A query plan, also known as an execution plan, is the blueprint that the database engine follows to execute a query. It includes details such as the order in which tables are accessed, the type of joins used, whether indexes are employed, the direction of index scans, the use of temporary or hash tables, and the application of filters. Query plans can be viewed in either graphical or textual formats, depending on the database system and tools used. These plans reveal not only the chosen execution path but also the estimated and actual row counts, allowing users to compare the optimizer's assumptions with real-world results.

When performance issues arise, examining the query plan is one of the most effective ways to identify inefficiencies. For instance, a query that unexpectedly performs a full table scan instead of using an index may point to missing or outdated statistics, or to a query predicate that is incompatible with the available indexes. Similarly, an unexpectedly expensive nested loop join may indicate that the optimizer underestimated the number of rows in one of the input tables. Understanding these indicators allows developers and administrators to take corrective action, such as updating statistics, modifying indexes, or rewriting queries.

Another important concept related to statistics and query plans is parameter sniffing. This occurs when a query uses a parameterized value and the optimizer generates a plan based on the value of the parameter at the time of compilation. If that parameter represents an atypical value, the resulting plan may be poorly suited to future executions with different parameters. This issue is common in stored procedures or prepared statements and can cause wide variations in performance. Techniques to mitigate parameter sniffing include using query hints, creating plan guides, or rewriting queries to use dynamic SQL that forces recompilation.

In systems with complex queries or large numbers of joins, query plan stability becomes a concern. A slight change in statistics or query syntax can cause the optimizer to choose a completely different plan, which may not perform as well. Some database engines offer plan freezing or plan forcing features that allow administrators to lock in a known good plan for critical queries. While this ensures consistent performance, it must be managed carefully to prevent outdated plans from degrading performance over time as data changes. Periodic review and testing of frozen plans are necessary to maintain their effectiveness.

The optimizer's behavior also varies based on configuration settings and the specific implementation in each database engine. For example, some systems use a cost-based optimizer exclusively, while others incorporate rule-based elements. Advanced optimizers may include machine learning models that learn from past execution results to improve future decisions. These features can enhance optimization over time, but they also introduce complexity that requires a deeper understanding of how the optimizer interprets statistics and adjusts plans.

Index selection is one of the most visible impacts of statistics on query plans. The optimizer uses column cardinality and distribution data to decide whether an index seek, index scan, or full table scan will be most efficient. It also considers the potential use of composite indexes and covering indexes. If statistics suggest that a filter will return a large percentage of rows, the optimizer may choose a scan rather than a seek, even if an index exists. This decision often surprises developers who assume that an index guarantees its use in every case. Accurate statistics are the only way for the optimizer to make such decisions wisely.

Database administrators and developers can benefit immensely from developing a strong understanding of the relationship between statistics and query plans. By regularly analyzing execution plans, updating statistics, and understanding the optimizer's decision-making process, they can fine-tune queries and indexes to ensure maximum efficiency. This proactive approach reduces the need for reactive troubleshooting and supports a more predictable and high-performing database environment. As data volumes grow and applications become more complex, mastering these foundational elements becomes increasingly important for delivering fast, reliable, and scalable systems.

The Role of the Query Optimizer

The query optimizer is one of the most sophisticated and essential components of a relational database management system. Its primary responsibility is to determine the most efficient way to execute a SQL query. When a query is submitted to the database, the optimizer evaluates multiple execution strategies and chooses the one with the lowest estimated cost, based on a combination of available statistics, indexing options, data distribution, and system configuration. This process is crucial for performance, as the difference between a well-optimized query and a poorly executed one can mean the difference between a response time of milliseconds and several minutes or even hours.

At a fundamental level, the optimizer functions as a decision-making engine. It does not execute the query itself but rather produces a plan that the database engine will follow during execution. This plan includes a detailed sequence of operations, such as which indexes to use, the order of joins, the join algorithms to apply, whether to use temporary storage, and the direction of data access. The optimizer's effectiveness is directly tied to its ability to make the right choices, which in turn depends on the accuracy and completeness of the statistical metadata it has at its disposal. These statistics provide critical insight into data distribution, table size, value frequency, and the uniqueness of columns, all of which influence how the optimizer estimates costs.

The optimizer must evaluate a vast search space of possible execution plans, especially for complex queries involving multiple joins, subqueries, groupings, and aggregations. To manage this complexity, most modern optimizers use a cost-based approach. They assign a cost to each possible execution path based on estimated resource usage, including CPU cycles, memory requirements, and disk I/O. The optimizer then selects the plan with the lowest total cost. While the exact formulas and weightings vary between database systems, the underlying principle remains the same: minimize resource consumption while preserving accuracy and completeness of the result.

For example, consider a query that retrieves customer orders from a table using a specific customer ID. The optimizer will evaluate whether a table scan or an index seek is more efficient. If the table has an index on the customer ID column and the statistics indicate that the filter will significantly reduce the number of rows returned, the optimizer will likely choose the index seek. However, if the statistics are outdated or the filter is not selective, it may incorrectly estimate that a scan is cheaper. This demonstrates how the optimizer's decisions hinge on the quality of its inputs. Inaccurate or stale statistics can lead to poor performance, even when appropriate indexes exist.

Join ordering is another area where the optimizer plays a crucial role. In a query with multiple joins, the order in which tables are joined can greatly affect performance. The optimizer evaluates the cardinality of each table and the selectivity of join conditions to determine the best join sequence. It also decides which join algorithms to use, such as nested loop joins, hash joins, or merge joins. Each algorithm has strengths and weaknesses depending on the size of the input sets and the nature of the join conditions. The optimizer's ability to choose the right algorithm can have a dramatic impact on the query's execution time.

The query optimizer also determines whether to use parallel execution plans, which break down a query into smaller tasks that can be executed simultaneously across multiple CPU cores. This can accelerate large queries, especially those involving full table scans or large aggregations. However, parallel plans introduce overhead in terms of coordination and resource management, so the optimizer must weigh the potential gains against the additional costs. It makes these decisions based on system configuration, available hardware resources, and the estimated cost of serial execution.

Another function of the optimizer is to rewrite queries internally for better performance. Known as query transformation, this process involves modifying the query syntax or structure without altering its logical meaning. For instance, the optimizer might rewrite a subquery into a join, flatten a nested query, or simplify expressions. These transformations allow the optimizer to take advantage of indexing opportunities or execute the query more efficiently. In some cases, the transformed version of a query performs orders of magnitude better than the original version, especially when the original structure hides optimization opportunities.

Query hints and plan guides provide ways for developers and administrators to influence the decisions made by the optimizer. While the optimizer is generally trusted to choose the best plan, there are scenarios where human insight or specific knowledge about data patterns can improve performance. Hints allow users to suggest or enforce certain choices, such as using a specific index or join method. Plan guides can lock in a particular execution plan for critical queries. These tools must be used carefully, as they override the optimizer's autonomy and can lead to suboptimal performance if not regularly reviewed and maintained.

The optimizer also plays a role in maintaining plan stability. Inconsistent performance due to changing execution plans is a common issue in dynamic environments. A plan that works well for one parameter value may perform poorly for another. This phenomenon, known as parameter sniffing, occurs when the optimizer compiles a plan based on the first value it encounters and reuses that plan for subsequent executions. While this improves compilation efficiency, it can lead to significant performance variability. Solutions include using query recompilation, optimizing for typical values, or implementing conditional logic to guide execution paths.

Advanced database systems are increasingly integrating adaptive and intelligent optimizers that can learn from past query executions. These adaptive optimizers adjust plans in real time based on actual runtime metrics, or they gather feedback to improve future optimization. Machine learning techniques are being introduced to refine cost models and better predict performance outcomes. These advancements mark a shift toward more autonomous optimization, where the system not only analyzes static metadata but also evolves its understanding based on workload behavior.

Understanding the role of the query optimizer is essential for anyone working with relational databases. It demystifies why certain queries perform well and others do not, and it provides the tools necessary to diagnose and resolve performance problems. A well-designed query executed with poor optimization can behave worse than a less efficient query written with an optimizer in mind. By aligning query design with optimization principles, leveraging statistics, and interpreting execution plans, developers and administrators can ensure that the database engine consistently executes queries with maximum efficiency. The optimizer is not merely a passive component but an active participant in every query's journey from syntax to execution. Its decisions shape the performance, scalability, and reliability of data systems across every industry and application.

Cost-Based vs Rule-Based Optimization

Cost-based and rule-based optimization represent two fundamentally different approaches to query optimization in relational database systems. Both strategies aim to determine the most efficient way to execute SQL queries, but they rely on contrasting methodologies. Rule-based optimization makes decisions based on a predefined set of rules that prioritize certain operations over others, independent of the data itself. In contrast, cost-based optimization evaluates multiple execution plans and chooses the one with the lowest estimated cost based on statistical data about the underlying database. Each approach has its own advantages and trade-offs, and understanding their inner workings is crucial for designing efficient databases and writing performant queries.

Rule-based optimization was the dominant method in early relational databases. In this approach, the optimizer uses a fixed hierarchy of rules to determine which execution plan to use. These rules are based on assumptions about performance characteristics. For example, a rule-based optimizer might always choose an index scan over a table scan, or prefer a nested loop join over a hash join. These decisions are made without considering actual table sizes, data distribution, or runtime conditions. The simplicity of this model makes it easy to understand and predict, which can be advantageous for developers trying to anticipate query behavior.

However, rule-based optimization is rigid and often results in suboptimal performance, particularly as data volumes grow or become more complex. Because it does not adapt to changes in data, a rule-based optimizer might make decisions that are efficient for small datasets but disastrous for large ones. For instance, always choosing an index scan might work well when indexes are small and selective, but could be significantly slower when the index contains a high percentage of the table's rows. The lack of flexibility in this model becomes a serious limitation in dynamic or rapidly evolving environments where query patterns and data volumes are in constant flux.

Cost-based optimization was developed to overcome the limitations of rule-based systems. In a cost-based optimizer, the database engine analyzes available statistics on data such as table cardinality, column distribution, index selectivity, and data skew. These statistics are then used to estimate the cost of various query execution strategies. The optimizer evaluates many possible plans, each representing a different way to access and join data, and assigns a cost score to each. The plan with the lowest estimated cost is selected for execution. This approach allows the optimizer to tailor its decisions to the specific characteristics of the data, resulting in more efficient execution paths.

The cost model used by a cost-based optimizer takes into account a wide range of factors. These include the number of rows expected to be read, the estimated number of I/O operations, the expected CPU usage, memory allocation, and the availability of indexes or statistics. The optimizer also considers join order, join methods, and whether parallel execution will benefit performance. Because of this detailed analysis, cost-based optimization can generate very different plans for the same query depending on the state of the data and the system. This adaptability is one of its greatest strengths, allowing databases to maintain good performance even as data changes over time.

Despite its advantages, cost-based optimization also presents challenges. One of the primary difficulties is the reliance on accurate and up-to-date statistics. If the statistics are outdated or missing, the optimizer's cost estimates will be inaccurate, potentially leading to poor plan selection. For example, if the optimizer believes that a table contains far fewer rows than it actually does, it might choose a join method that performs well on small datasets but scales poorly with large ones. Keeping statistics current is therefore critical in cost-based systems, and many modern databases include automatic mechanisms to update them as data changes.

Another challenge is the complexity of the optimization process itself. Because the optimizer must evaluate many different execution paths, cost-based optimization can be computationally intensive, especially for complex queries involving multiple joins, subqueries, or aggregations. To manage this, most systems implement heuristics to limit the number of plans considered or to prune obviously poor options early in the process. While these heuristics improve optimization speed, they can also lead to missed opportunities if a viable plan is excluded from evaluation due to time constraints.

Some systems support a hybrid approach, combining elements of both rule-based and cost-based optimization. In such systems, certain operations might be governed by rules, particularly when statistics are missing or unreliable, while others follow cost-based logic when sufficient data is available. This hybrid model provides a fallback mechanism and ensures that the database remains operational even in suboptimal conditions. However, it also introduces additional complexity and makes it more difficult to predict how a query will be optimized.

The transition from rule-based to cost-based optimization marked a significant evolution in database technology. As systems became more sophisticated and the volume of data increased, the need for adaptive, data-aware optimization strategies became evident. Cost-based optimizers are now the standard in modern relational databases, including systems such as Oracle, SQL Server, PostgreSQL, MySQL, and many others. Their ability to make intelligent decisions based on the actual characteristics of data enables better performance, reduced resource consumption, and more consistent user experiences.

Understanding the difference between these two optimization strategies also helps explain why query performance can vary across environments or even within the same environment over time. A query that runs quickly in a development database may perform poorly in production if the underlying data characteristics differ. Similarly, a query may run efficiently one day and slow down the next if large volumes of new data are added or if indexes are dropped or altered. In such cases, reviewing execution plans and analyzing the optimizer's decisions often reveals the root cause of the performance change.

For developers and database administrators, learning how to read execution plans and understand the optimizer's choices is a valuable skill. It enables them to identify when the optimizer has made a poor decision, and whether that decision was caused by inaccurate statistics, missing indexes, or an overly complex query structure. Tuning queries in cost-based systems often involves not just rewriting the SQL, but also improving the data model, creating or adjusting indexes, and ensuring that statistics reflect the current state of the data.

Ultimately, cost-based optimization represents a more intelligent and flexible approach to query execution, but it requires more sophisticated system design and maintenance practices. Rule-based optimization, while easier to understand and predict, lacks the adaptability necessary for handling modern workloads. Both models reflect different stages in the evolution of database technology, and both continue to inform best practices in query tuning and system optimization. As data continues to grow in complexity and volume, the importance of a well-functioning optimizer becomes ever more central to the success of any data-driven application or enterprise system.

Writing Efficient SQL Queries

Writing efficient SQL queries is one of the most impactful skills a developer or database administrator can possess. A well-written query can return results in milliseconds and scale smoothly with increasing data volume, while a poorly written one can cause performance bottlenecks, consume excessive system resources, and frustrate users with slow response times. SQL, being a declarative language, allows users to express what data they want without specifying how to retrieve it. However, despite its simplicity on the surface, the way a query is written has a profound influence on how the database engine processes it. Understanding the internal mechanisms of the database and aligning queries with those mechanisms is the key to unlocking high performance.

An efficient query begins with clarity of purpose and a solid understanding of the underlying schema. Knowing how tables are structured, how they relate to each other through primary and foreign keys, and which columns are indexed forms the foundation for constructing a performant query. Queries that reflect the logical structure of the schema and leverage indexing appropriately reduce the amount of data scanned and improve the accuracy of execution plans. It is critical to write queries that are selective, meaning they reduce the result set as early as possible in the query's logical flow, minimizing the number of rows that must be processed in later stages.

One of the most common causes of inefficient queries is the use of non-sargable expressions, which prevent the use of indexes. A query is sargable when it allows the optimizer to use an index to quickly locate rows, typically by comparing columns to constant values or parameters using operators such as equals, greater than, or less than. Expressions that apply functions or mathematical operations directly to columns, such as WHERE YEAR(order_date) = 2023, force the database to evaluate the expression for each row, effectively disabling the use of indexes and triggering a full table scan. Rewriting such conditions to preserve index usage, such as WHERE order_date >= '2023-01-01' AND order_date < '2024-01-01', significantly improves performance.

Join operations are another area where efficiency can vary greatly depending on query structure. Understanding the type of join being used and the expected number of rows returned from each table is essential. Nested loop joins, hash joins, and merge joins each perform differently under different conditions. When writing queries with multiple joins, the order and type of each join should align with the volume of data and the selectivity of filters. Placing the most selective joins or filters earlier in the logical flow can reduce the number of rows passed on to subsequent joins. Including only the necessary tables and avoiding unnecessary joins helps reduce complexity and improve performance.

Efficient SQL also involves minimizing the data retrieved. Using SELECT * retrieves all columns from a table, many of which may not be needed for the task at hand. This not only wastes bandwidth and memory but can also prevent the use of covering indexes. Explicitly specifying only the required columns ensures that the database processes less data and enables the optimizer to choose more efficient execution strategies. Similarly, filtering results as early as possible using WHERE clauses and avoiding post-processing filters in the application logic helps offload work to the database engine, which is optimized for such operations.

Another performance pitfall is the use of correlated subqueries, which execute once for every row in the outer query. In cases where the same result could be obtained using a join or a window function, rewriting the query to eliminate the correlated subquery can dramatically reduce execution time. For example, retrieving the most recent order for each customer can be done using a subquery correlated on customer ID, but using a window function with ROW_NUMBER() or RANK() often provides a more efficient and scalable solution.

Aggregation operations such as GROUP BY and DISTINCT should also be used thoughtfully. These operations require sorting or hashing and are often resource-intensive. When aggregating data, including only the necessary columns in the GROUP BY clause and applying filters before aggregation reduces the amount of data that needs to be grouped. In some cases, it is possible to use indexed views or pre-aggregated summary tables to speed up repetitive aggregation queries, especially in analytical workloads.

Efficient query writing also involves anticipating how the optimizer interprets the query. Even semantically equivalent queries can generate different execution plans depending on syntax. For instance, using IN versus EXISTS or a JOIN can lead to different plans with varying performance characteristics depending on the data involved.

Testing different forms of the same query and analyzing their execution plans helps identify which version performs best under current conditions. Understanding how the optimizer rewrites and transforms queries allows developers to write SQL that guides the optimizer toward efficient paths.

Pagination and limit-based retrieval are additional areas where query efficiency matters. Using OFFSET with large values causes the database to scan and skip over a large number of rows before returning the desired result, which can be very slow in large datasets. Alternatives such as keyset pagination, where the last-seen value is used to retrieve the next set of results, are more efficient and scale better. This approach avoids skipping rows and leverages indexes effectively, providing faster response times and reduced server load.

Query efficiency is also affected by transaction context and isolation level. Long-running queries that lock rows or hold resources can interfere with concurrent operations, leading to contention and deadlocks. Writing queries that are short, precise, and executed within well-scoped transactions helps maintain system stability and responsiveness. Additionally, understanding the isolation level used and how it affects locking and consistency ensures that queries do not inadvertently block each other or return stale data.

Finally, efficient SQL is not just about writing code that runs fast today but about building queries that remain performant as data grows. This requires a mindset of proactive tuning, regular analysis of execution plans, and ongoing collaboration with the database infrastructure. Query performance should be validated in environments that reflect production data volumes and access patterns. Continuous profiling and performance monitoring allow developers to spot regressions and adapt queries to evolving requirements. Writing efficient SQL is both a science and an art, demanding a deep understanding of database internals, attention to detail, and a commitment to long-term maintainability.

Joins and Subqueries Optimization

Optimizing joins and subqueries is essential for achieving high-performance SQL queries in relational database systems. These constructs are among the most powerful features of SQL, allowing developers to retrieve data from multiple tables or derive complex result sets from nested logic. However, they also introduce layers of complexity that can significantly affect performance if not carefully managed. Understanding how the database processes joins and subqueries, and how the query optimizer interprets them, provides the foundation for writing efficient and scalable queries. As data volumes increase and business logic becomes more sophisticated, join and subquery optimization becomes not only a matter of speed but a prerequisite for system stability and responsiveness.

Joins are used to combine data from two or more tables based on a related column, and they come in various types, including inner joins, left joins, right joins, and full outer joins. The performance of a join depends on several factors, including the size of the input tables, the availability of indexes, the selectivity of the join conditions, and the type of join algorithm chosen by the optimizer. The optimizer decides between join methods such as nested loop joins, hash joins, and merge joins based on estimated costs derived from statistics. Nested loop joins are efficient when one of the inputs is small and well-indexed, while hash joins are better suited for large, unsorted data sets. Merge joins require both inputs to be sorted and can perform well in sorted environments, especially with indexes that support ordered scans.

To optimize joins, it is crucial to understand the order in which they are executed. The optimizer may reorder join operations to minimize the size of intermediate result sets. However, developers can help the optimizer by filtering rows as early as possible in the query, thereby reducing the number of rows passed into joins. Applying WHERE clauses to limit rows before the join operations occur can drastically reduce memory usage and processing time. Another important consideration is join selectivity. When joining two tables, the column used for the join should ideally be highly selective, meaning it matches only a small percentage of rows. Joining on low-cardinality columns can lead to large intermediate result sets and poor performance.

Indexes play a critical role in join optimization. When appropriate indexes exist on join keys, the database can use index seeks instead of scans, significantly improving performance. For example, joining a large orders table to a smaller customers table on customer_id becomes faster when the customer_id column is indexed in both tables. In some cases, the use of a covering index can eliminate the need to access the base table altogether, making the join operation even more efficient. Monitoring execution plans helps identify whether indexes are being used effectively and whether additional indexes should be created or existing ones adjusted.

Subqueries, which are queries nested inside other queries, offer a powerful way to express logic that depends on intermediate or derived results. They can appear in SELECT, FROM, or WHERE clauses and can be either correlated or uncorrelated. Correlated subqueries reference columns from the outer query and are evaluated once for each row of the outer query. This repeated evaluation can become a major performance bottleneck, especially if the subquery involves a scan or complex logic. Uncorrelated subqueries, in contrast, are evaluated only once and are generally more efficient. One of the most effective ways to optimize correlated subqueries is to rewrite them as joins. In many cases, the same result can be achieved more efficiently with a join, which allows the optimizer to treat the query as a single relational expression and apply optimizations like predicate pushdown and join reordering.

For instance, a query that retrieves all employees who have received bonuses by using a correlated subquery can often be rewritten using an inner join with the bonuses table. This not only improves performance but also makes the query easier to understand and maintain. Similarly, subqueries in the SELECT clause that compute scalar values can often be replaced by derived tables or common table expressions, allowing the optimizer to better estimate cardinality and costs.

IN, EXISTS, ANY, and ALL are logical operators commonly used with subqueries and can affect performance differently depending on the context. The EXISTS operator typically performs better than IN when the subquery returns many rows, as it stops scanning as soon as a match is found. Conversely, IN may be more efficient when the subquery returns a small, static list. Understanding the behavior of these operators helps in choosing the right approach for each scenario. Additionally, some databases optimize these constructs internally, transforming them into joins during query compilation. Reviewing the execution plan reveals how the database interprets and processes subqueries, offering insight into possible rewrites for better performance.

Subqueries in the FROM clause, also known as derived tables, can also be optimized by materializing the result set before the main query executes. However, in some systems, the optimizer may not be able to push filters into the subquery or reuse indexes unless the subquery is simplified or rewritten. Using common table expressions, or CTEs, can sometimes help clarify the query structure but may also lead to performance issues if not used carefully. In particular, recursive CTEs and complex nested CTEs can produce inefficient plans or consume excessive memory if the intermediate results are large.

The key to optimizing joins and subqueries lies in a deep understanding of how the database engine processes queries and the ability to read and interpret execution plans. Index usage, row estimates, join orders, and access methods are all visible in the plan and indicate whether the optimizer's choices align with expectations. When the plan deviates from the optimal path, the root cause is often inaccurate statistics, missing indexes, or suboptimal query structure. Updating statistics, creating appropriate indexes, and restructuring the query can correct these inefficiencies and restore performance.

Efficient joins and subqueries are also important for scalability. As data grows, queries that were once fast can slow down dramatically if they are not designed to scale. Writing queries that minimize row scans, limit intermediate result sizes, and exploit indexes ensures that performance remains acceptable even under increasing load. Testing queries against large datasets and monitoring them in production environments helps validate their scalability. In systems that support query profiling and monitoring tools, capturing metrics such as execution time, CPU usage, and I/O reads provides a detailed view of query performance and reveals opportunities for improvement.

Developing efficient join and subquery logic is an iterative process. It involves not only writing the initial SQL but continually refining it based on actual data and query behavior. As schemas evolve and new requirements emerge, existing queries must be revisited and tuned to maintain optimal performance. Mastery of join and subquery optimization leads to more responsive applications, better resource utilization, and a more predictable database environment. It allows developers and administrators to confidently support growing workloads and deliver the level of performance users expect in modern data-driven systems.

Understanding Execution Plans

Understanding execution plans is essential for diagnosing and improving SQL query performance in relational database systems. An execution plan, also known as a query plan, is a detailed roadmap that shows how the database engine will retrieve the data requested in a SQL statement. Rather than executing the query as it is written, the database translates the SQL into a series of internal operations that follow a logical sequence, and the execution plan documents this sequence. This plan includes decisions such as which indexes to use, what type of join algorithms to apply, how to scan tables, and the order in which operations will be executed. By analyzing the execution plan, developers and administrators can uncover inefficiencies and optimize their queries to perform faster and more reliably.

Execution plans are generated by the query optimizer, which is responsible for evaluating various possible methods for executing a query and selecting the one with the lowest estimated cost. This cost is a relative value based on internal calculations involving CPU cycles, I/O operations, memory usage, and network activity. The optimizer examines metadata such as table statistics, available indexes, and data distribution to estimate how many rows each operation will process. The accuracy of these estimates directly influences the quality of the execution plan. When statistics are outdated or missing, the optimizer may choose an inefficient path, which results in slower query performance.

There are typically two forms of execution plans available to users: estimated execution plans and actual execution plans. The estimated plan is generated before the query runs and is based solely on statistics. It provides insight into how the optimizer thinks the query will behave. The actual plan, on the other hand, is generated during execution and includes real runtime metrics such as the number of rows processed by each step and the actual time taken. Comparing these two plans can highlight discrepancies between expectation and reality, revealing issues such as underestimation of row counts or missed index usage.

Execution plans are composed of a hierarchy of operators, each representing a single step in the data retrieval process. These operators include index seeks, index scans, table scans, joins, sorts, aggregates, filters, and more. At the top of the plan is the root node, which typically represents the final output operation, such as returning rows to the client. Each child node feeds data into its parent, forming a tree structure. Understanding the flow of data through this tree helps identify bottlenecks and opportunities for improvement.

Index seeks are one of the most desirable operations in a plan, indicating that the query is using an index to quickly locate specific rows. Index scans are less efficient but still preferable to full table scans when the index covers the required columns. A full table scan, or clustered index scan in the case of tables with clustered indexes, reads every row in the table and is generally a sign that better indexing or filtering is needed. Joins in the plan can take the form of nested loops, hash joins, or merge joins, and the choice of join algorithm is based on estimated row counts and data ordering. Nested loop joins are ideal for small input sets with good indexing, hash joins work well with large, unsorted datasets, and merge joins are efficient for sorted inputs.

One common performance problem revealed in execution plans is the presence of expensive sort operations. When a query includes an ORDER BY or GROUP BY clause without an appropriate index, the database must sort the data explicitly. This operation can consume a significant amount of memory and CPU, particularly if the sort spills to disk due to insufficient memory. The plan will indicate whether a sort occurred, how much memory was used, and whether the operation was completed in memory or required temporary disk storage. Creating indexes that support the desired sort order can eliminate these expensive operations and speed up query performance.

Another frequent issue involves residual predicates. These appear when the optimizer uses an index that does not completely filter the data and applies additional filtering after the index operation. While this is sometimes necessary, it often signals that the index is not fully aligned with the query conditions. The execution plan will show a filter operation that occurs after the index seek or scan, indicating that the engine is doing extra work to discard rows. Adjusting the index to better match the query can reduce the need for post-processing filters.

Execution plans also reveal the use of lookups, particularly key lookups in clustered tables. A key lookup occurs when a non-covering index is used to find matching rows, but the query requires additional columns not included in the index. The database retrieves the matching keys from the index and then looks up the full row in the clustered index. This operation can be expensive when performed many times, especially if the lookup results in random I/O. Creating a covering index that includes all columns used in the query can eliminate the need for lookups and improve performance.

Parallelism is another aspect of execution plans that can significantly affect query behavior. When the database decides to execute a query using multiple threads, the plan will include operators related to parallel processing. These include distribute streams, gather streams, and repartition operations. While parallelism can improve performance for large queries, it also introduces overhead and can consume more CPU. Plans showing parallel operations should be examined to ensure that the benefits outweigh the costs and that the server has sufficient resources to handle concurrent parallel queries.

Understanding execution plans also means being able to detect plan regressions. A plan regression occurs when a previously efficient query begins to perform poorly because the optimizer has chosen a different, less optimal plan. This can happen due to changes in data distribution, outdated statistics, or structural changes in the schema. Regularly reviewing execution plans for critical queries helps detect regressions early. Some database systems offer plan caching and baselines to preserve known good plans, but relying on these features without understanding the underlying causes of regressions can lead to long-term inefficiencies.

Tools for viewing and analyzing execution plans vary between platforms but generally include graphical and text-based options. Graphical plans are easier to interpret visually and help spot expensive operations quickly, often highlighting them with color or icons. Text plans provide a detailed, sequential view of each operator and its estimated and actual performance. Both formats include valuable data such as estimated rows, actual rows, estimated I/O, CPU cost, and memory usage. Learning to interpret these values and relate them to query logic is an essential skill for performance tuning.

Developers and administrators who understand execution plans are better equipped to write efficient queries, design effective indexes, and maintain database performance over time. They can identify the exact cause of slow queries, validate the effectiveness of tuning efforts, and make data-driven decisions to improve application responsiveness. Execution plans are not just diagnostic tools; they are blueprints that reveal how the database engine thinks and behaves. Mastering their interpretation is a powerful step toward building faster, smarter, and more reliable database systems.

Caching and Buffer Pool Management

Caching and buffer pool management are critical components of a relational database engine that directly influence performance, responsiveness, and resource efficiency. Every database system relies on a complex memory management mechanism to reduce the cost of disk I/O operations, which are typically slower than memory access. By leveraging memory to temporarily store frequently accessed data pages, execution plans, and query results, a database can serve repeated requests significantly faster than if it had to retrieve the same data from storage on every access. Understanding how caching and buffer pools function, and how they are managed by the database, allows administrators and developers to tune systems effectively, avoid bottlenecks, and maximize throughput.

The buffer pool, also referred to as the buffer cache, is the memory area used by the database engine to store pages read from disk. These pages include data rows, index pages, system metadata, and temporary structures needed for processing complex queries. When a query requests data, the database first checks whether the required page is already in the buffer pool. If it is found, this is called a buffer cache hit, and the data is returned directly from memory. If it is not found, a cache miss occurs, prompting the database to read the page from disk and place it in the buffer pool before serving it to the query engine. The hit ratio, which measures the proportion of cache hits to total requests, is a key performance indicator for buffer pool efficiency. A high hit ratio usually means the system is effectively utilizing memory and minimizing slow disk reads.

The size of the buffer pool is a configurable parameter and plays a major role in overall system performance. If the buffer pool is too small relative to the size and activity of the database, the system will frequently evict pages to make room for new ones, causing more cache misses and degrading performance. On the other hand, allocating too much memory to the buffer pool at the expense of other processes can lead to contention and instability at the operating system level. The optimal buffer pool size depends on available hardware, workload patterns, data size, and access frequency. Modern databases may support dynamic resizing of the buffer pool, adapting to changing workload demands without requiring manual reconfiguration or restart.

To determine which pages remain in the buffer pool and which are evicted, the database uses an internal page replacement algorithm. The most common algorithms are variants of least recently used, such as LRU or LRU-K, which track access history to prioritize keeping frequently or recently used pages in memory. These algorithms attempt to maintain a balance between short-term and long-term relevance, ensuring that hot pages are quickly accessible while less frequently accessed data is replaced over time. The effectiveness of the replacement strategy influences how well the buffer pool adapts to changing access patterns and maintains a high hit ratio.

In addition to the main buffer pool, databases often use separate caches for other purposes. These include the plan cache, which stores compiled query execution plans to avoid the overhead of recompiling them on repeated executions, and the result cache, which stores the final results of certain queries for faster response to identical requests.

Plan caching is particularly beneficial for complex queries with expensive compilation processes or parameterized queries that are executed frequently with different values. Effective use of plan caching reduces CPU usage and improves throughput, but it must be managed carefully to avoid bloating the cache with outdated or rarely used plans.

Buffer pool management also includes mechanisms for tracking and flushing dirty pages. A dirty page is one that has been modified in memory but not yet written back to disk. To ensure durability and data consistency, the database periodically flushes dirty pages from the buffer pool to disk. This operation is managed by a background writer process or checkpoint mechanism, which writes batches of dirty pages to disk based on thresholds or timed intervals. Frequent writes increase I/O load and reduce system responsiveness, while infrequent writes may delay data durability and increase recovery time in case of failure. Proper tuning of checkpoint frequency, write-ahead logging, and flushing behavior is essential for maintaining the balance between performance and reliability.

Concurrency is another factor affected by buffer pool management. When multiple sessions attempt to access or modify the same data pages, the database must coordinate access to ensure consistency. This often involves acquiring latches or lightweight locks on buffer pool pages, which can become a source of contention under high concurrency. Buffer pool partitioning or multibuffer pools can help reduce contention by distributing access across multiple memory regions. These techniques improve scalability and enable the system to handle large numbers of concurrent queries without performance degradation.

Monitoring and diagnostics tools provided by the database can reveal detailed metrics about the buffer pool's behavior. These metrics include the number of page reads, writes, cache hits, and misses, as well as memory usage by each component of the cache. Observing trends in these metrics helps identify issues such as poor index design, inefficient query patterns, or insufficient memory allocation. For example, a sudden drop in cache hit ratio may indicate that a new query or report is accessing large amounts of previously unused data, or that a recent change in indexing has altered access patterns.

Caching strategies also play an important role in distributed and cloud-native database architectures. In such environments, multiple nodes may share data storage but have separate local caches. Coordinating cache invalidation, replication, and consistency across nodes becomes more complex, especially when data is updated concurrently. Some distributed systems implement shared cache layers or use in-memory data grids to provide faster access to commonly used data across nodes. Others rely on hybrid approaches, combining local buffer pools with global caching mechanisms to balance latency, consistency, and fault tolerance.

In-memory databases take the concept of caching to the extreme by storing all or most of the database contents in RAM. These systems eliminate the distinction between disk and buffer pool, delivering ultra-fast data access but requiring careful memory management to avoid data loss and ensure persistence through snapshotting or logging. While in-memory databases are ideal for high-throughput applications with real-time requirements, they still benefit from traditional buffer management techniques to handle temporary data, intermediate results, and background tasks efficiently.

Ultimately, the effectiveness of caching and buffer pool management defines the performance boundaries of any database system. By reducing disk I/O, optimizing memory usage, and adapting to workload patterns, the buffer pool acts as a high-speed intermediary between slow storage and fast processors. A well-tuned buffer pool increases throughput, reduces query latency, and ensures consistent performance under varying loads. Deep knowledge of how the buffer pool operates empowers administrators to make informed decisions about configuration, indexing, and query design, leading to more resilient, faster, and scalable database environments.

Locking and Concurrency Control

Locking and concurrency control are foundational components of relational database systems that ensure consistency, correctness, and isolation when multiple transactions access the database simultaneously. In a multi-user environment, where numerous operations are executed concurrently, it is vital to prevent conflicts that could lead to data corruption, lost updates, or inconsistent reads. To address these challenges, databases implement locking mechanisms and concurrency control protocols that coordinate access to data, preserving the integrity of transactions while maintaining acceptable levels of performance and throughput. These mechanisms must strike a balance between isolation and concurrency, ensuring that one transaction's view of the data is not adversely affected by others, without unnecessarily blocking or delaying operations.

At its core, a lock is a mechanism that restricts access to a resource. In databases, this typically means placing a temporary hold on rows, pages, or even entire tables to prevent other transactions from making changes that could interfere with the current operation. Locks can be either shared or exclusive. A shared lock allows multiple transactions to read a resource but prevents any of them from modifying it. An exclusive lock, in contrast, prevents all other access—both reads and writes—until the lock is released. These locking modes form the basis of a broader system known as two-phase locking, which is the most widely used concurrency control protocol in relational databases.

The two-phase locking protocol ensures serializability, the highest level of isolation, by dividing the transaction's life into two distinct phases. During the growing phase, the transaction can acquire new locks but cannot release any. Once it releases its first lock, it enters the shrinking phase and can no longer obtain new locks. This structure prevents cyclic dependencies and guarantees that transactions execute in an order that is equivalent to some serial execution, preserving consistency. However, strict adherence to this protocol can introduce contention and reduce concurrency, especially in systems with a high volume of simultaneous updates.

To reduce contention and improve concurrency, databases often provide multiple isolation levels, each offering a different balance between consistency and performance. The most common isolation levels are Read Uncommitted, Read Committed, Repeatable Read, and Serializable. Read Uncommitted permits the highest degree of concurrency by allowing transactions to read data that has not yet been committed by other transactions, but it risks dirty reads. Read Committed, the default in many systems, prevents dirty reads by ensuring that no transaction can read data written by an uncommitted transaction. Repeatable Read prevents non-repeatable reads by maintaining locks on read data until the transaction completes, while Serializable ensures full isolation by treating transactions as if they were executed one at a time. Each level increases in isolation and locking overhead, and choosing the appropriate level depends on the specific requirements of the application.

Deadlocks are a common issue in systems that use locking for concurrency control. A deadlock occurs when two or more transactions hold locks that the others need in order to proceed, creating a circular wait that prevents any of them from completing. Databases use deadlock detection algorithms to identify such conditions and resolve them by rolling back one of the transactions, allowing the others to continue. While deadlocks are inevitable in some scenarios, they can be minimized by following consistent locking order practices, keeping transactions short, and accessing resources in a predictable sequence.

Row-level locking offers fine-grained control and allows many users to access different parts of a table simultaneously. This increases concurrency but also introduces higher overhead due to the large number of locks the system must track. Page-level locking, which locks an entire block of data pages, offers a compromise between concurrency and overhead. Table-level locking is the most restrictive, blocking access to the entire table during a transaction. While this can simplify processing and avoid certain conflicts, it greatly reduces concurrency and is only suitable for specific use cases such as bulk updates or schema changes.

Databases also implement lock escalation, a process where the system automatically replaces multiple fine-grained locks with a single coarser-grained lock when a transaction acquires too many locks. This helps manage memory and reduce lock management overhead, but it can lead to contention if other transactions are affected by the escalated lock. Monitoring lock escalation and configuring thresholds accordingly is important for avoiding unnecessary contention in high-throughput systems.

In addition to traditional pessimistic locking, many modern databases support optimistic concurrency control. In this model, the system assumes that conflicts are rare and allows transactions to proceed without acquiring locks. At commit time, the system checks whether any conflicts occurred by comparing the current state of the data to the state it was in when the transaction began. If a conflict is detected, the transaction is rolled back. Optimistic control is especially useful in read-heavy environments with infrequent updates, as it avoids the overhead of locking and allows for greater concurrency.

Another advanced technique is multiversion concurrency control, or MVCC. MVCC allows transactions to read from snapshots of the data, enabling readers and writers to operate concurrently without blocking each other. When a transaction begins, it sees a consistent snapshot of the database as it existed at that point in time. Writers, meanwhile, create new versions of rows rather than modifying existing ones, and these versions are made visible only when the transaction commits. This model reduces contention and improves performance in systems with high read activity. However, MVCC also requires the database to manage and eventually clean up old row versions, which adds complexity to the system.

Effective concurrency control also involves transaction design. Long-running transactions are more likely to hold locks for extended periods, increasing the risk of blocking and deadlocks. Breaking up large operations into smaller, independent transactions can reduce lock duration and improve overall system throughput. Additionally, ensuring that transactions touch only the necessary data helps minimize the number of locks acquired and the potential for conflict.

Monitoring tools are essential for diagnosing and tuning concurrency issues. Databases provide dynamic views and logs that show which sessions are holding locks, waiting on locks, or contributing to blocking chains. By analyzing these reports, administrators can identify problem queries, index strategies, or transaction patterns that lead to contention. In some cases, application-level changes, such as modifying the order in which resources are accessed or batching operations differently, can resolve underlying concurrency problems.

Locking and concurrency control are at the heart of reliable database systems. They provide the mechanisms that make simultaneous access safe and predictable while allowing systems to scale with user demand. By understanding how locking works, choosing the appropriate isolation levels, designing efficient transactions, and monitoring system behavior, developers and administrators can ensure that their databases remain fast, consistent, and resilient under concurrent workloads. These practices lead to better performance, fewer conflicts, and a smoother experience for users who depend on real-time access to accurate data.

Transactions and Isolation Levels

Transactions are a fundamental concept in relational database systems, designed to ensure that operations on data are executed in a reliable, consistent, and isolated manner. A transaction is a sequence of one or more operations that are treated as a single logical unit of work. Transactions provide critical guarantees that allow databases to handle multiple concurrent operations without compromising data integrity. These guarantees are encapsulated in the ACID properties: atomicity, consistency, isolation, and durability. Among these, isolation plays a central role in defining how transactions interact with each other, making isolation levels a core element of database behavior and performance.

Atomicity ensures that all the operations within a transaction are completed successfully, or none are applied at all. This prevents the database from being left in a partially updated state in the event of an error or interruption. Consistency guarantees that a transaction takes the database from one valid state to another, enforcing all defined rules and constraints. Durability ensures that once a transaction commits, its changes are permanent and survive system crashes. Isolation, perhaps the most complex of the four, determines how the database manages concurrent execution of transactions and whether the operations within one transaction are visible to others before the transaction completes.

The level of isolation directly affects the phenomena that can occur during concurrent transaction execution. These phenomena include dirty reads, non-repeatable reads, and phantom reads. A dirty read happens when a transaction reads data that has been written by another transaction but not yet committed. If the writing transaction rolls back, the data read by the first transaction becomes invalid. A non-repeatable read occurs when a transaction reads the same row twice and finds different values because another transaction has modified the data in the interim. A phantom read involves a transaction reading a set of rows that match a condition, then re-reading with the same condition and finding additional rows that have been inserted by another transaction.

To control these anomalies, relational databases offer several isolation levels defined by the SQL standard. These are Read Uncommitted, Read Committed, Repeatable Read, and Serializable. Each level offers a different trade-off between data integrity and system performance, with higher levels providing more isolation but incurring greater locking overhead and potential contention.

Read Uncommitted is the lowest isolation level, allowing transactions to read data that other transactions have written but not yet committed. This level offers maximum concurrency but allows dirty reads, which can compromise data correctness. It is rarely suitable for critical transactional operations but may be useful in analytical or monitoring scenarios where data consistency is less critical and performance is paramount.

Read Committed is the most commonly used isolation level and the default in many database systems. It prevents dirty reads by ensuring that a transaction can only read data that has been committed. This is achieved by acquiring shared locks during read operations and releasing them immediately after the read. While this prevents transactions from reading uncommitted changes, it does not protect against non-repeatable reads or phantom reads. A row read earlier in the transaction might be changed by another transaction before the current one finishes, potentially leading to inconsistencies if the same row is read again.

Repeatable Read provides a higher level of isolation by preventing both dirty and non-repeatable reads. It ensures that if a transaction reads a row once, it will see the same value if it reads that row again, even if another transaction updates the row in the meantime. This is accomplished by holding read locks on all rows accessed for the duration of the transaction. However, Repeatable Read does not prevent phantom reads, where new rows are added by other transactions that meet the conditions of a previous query. To prevent phantoms, the next level of isolation is required.

Serializable is the highest standard isolation level and provides full isolation between transactions. It ensures that the outcome of executing transactions concurrently is the same as if they were executed one at a time in some serial order. Serializable prevents dirty reads, non-repeatable reads, and phantom reads by using a combination of locking and range scans that lock entire sets of data. While this level offers the most robust protection against concurrency anomalies, it can significantly reduce system throughput due to increased lock contention and blocking. Serializable isolation is best suited for operations that require strict accuracy and consistency, such as financial calculations or batch processing.

Some modern databases implement Serializable isolation using techniques like snapshot isolation or multiversion concurrency control, which avoid locking by maintaining multiple versions of data. These techniques allow transactions to work on consistent snapshots of the database while still enabling high concurrency. Although they are logically equivalent to Serializable isolation in terms of preventing anomalies, their implementation differs and may introduce other trade-offs, such as increased memory usage or longer transaction validation phases.

Choosing the appropriate isolation level requires understanding the needs of the application and the behavior of the data. Higher isolation levels improve data consistency but increase the risk of blocking, deadlocks, and performance degradation. Lower isolation levels allow greater concurrency but expose transactions to inconsistencies. For many applications, Read Committed offers a good balance between consistency and performance. However, for use cases that require reliable and repeatable results, such as long-running reports or critical updates, higher isolation levels like Repeatable Read or Serializable may be necessary.

Isolation levels can be configured globally or specified per transaction, giving developers and administrators control over concurrency behavior. In dynamic systems, tuning isolation levels dynamically based on workload characteristics can optimize both performance and correctness. Monitoring tools and transaction diagnostics help identify issues such as long-running locks, blocking chains, and contention hotspots, which may indicate that the current isolation level is either too strict or too permissive for the workload.

Effective use of transactions and isolation levels is essential for building reliable and performant database systems. Transactions provide the structure and safety required for consistent data management, while isolation levels give the flexibility needed to balance integrity with scalability. Understanding how these elements interact enables developers to write better queries, design safer applications, and avoid subtle bugs that may only surface under concurrent load. In any multi-user system, the way transactions and isolation are handled determines not only the accuracy of the data but also the responsiveness and stability of the application as a whole.

Deadlocks and Their Resolution

Deadlocks are a critical concern in the design and operation of relational database systems, especially in environments that support high levels of concurrency. A deadlock occurs when two or more transactions are each waiting for resources that the other transactions have locked, creating a cycle of dependencies that prevents any of them from proceeding. In this state, each transaction is waiting for the other to release a lock, but none can continue because doing so requires access to a locked resource. Without intervention, this cycle continues indefinitely, effectively halting the progress of all involved transactions. Deadlocks are not inherently errors in logic, but they are failures in scheduling and resource allocation that must be resolved to maintain system responsiveness and data integrity.

Understanding how deadlocks form requires an awareness of the database locking mechanisms and how transactions interact with shared resources. In a typical scenario, Transaction A locks Row X and then attempts to lock Row Y, which is already locked by Transaction B. At the same time, Transaction B holds a lock on Row Y and tries to acquire a lock on Row X. Because both transactions are holding locks and simultaneously requesting locks held by the other, they become stuck in a circular wait condition. This classic deadlock scenario highlights the importance of resource access patterns and the sequence in which locks are acquired during a transaction's execution.

The conditions necessary for a deadlock to occur are well understood. These include mutual exclusion, where a resource is held exclusively by one transaction at a time; hold and wait, where a transaction holds one resource while waiting for others; no preemption, where a resource can only be released voluntarily by the holding transaction; and circular wait, where a closed chain of transactions exists such that each transaction holds at least one resource needed by the next transaction in the chain. If all these conditions are present simultaneously, a deadlock is possible.

To prevent deadlocks from degrading system performance, database management systems employ various strategies for detection and resolution. One common approach is deadlock detection through wait-for graphs. The system maintains a graph of transactions and the resources they are waiting for, checking periodically for cycles. If a cycle is detected, the system identifies it as a deadlock and selects one transaction to terminate, freeing its resources so that the other transactions can proceed. The selection of the victim transaction is typically based on criteria such as the transaction's age, the amount of work it has performed, or the likelihood of being rolled back successfully with minimal disruption.

When a deadlock is detected and a victim transaction is chosen, that transaction is rolled back, its locks are released, and an error is returned to the client. This interruption allows the remaining transactions in the deadlock cycle to continue. Although rolling back a transaction may seem drastic, it is a necessary measure to restore system progress. Well-designed applications should anticipate this possibility and implement retry logic for transactions that fail due to deadlocks. This enables the application to gracefully recover and retry the operation without user intervention, ensuring a better experience and maintaining data consistency.

Another approach to handling deadlocks is deadlock prevention, which involves designing transaction logic in such a way that deadlocks cannot occur. This can be achieved by enforcing a strict ordering on resource acquisition. If all transactions acquire locks in a predefined order, circular wait conditions cannot arise. For example, if all transactions first acquire a lock on the customer table before acquiring a lock on the orders table, they will not form a circular wait, even under high concurrency. However, enforcing such orderings may be difficult in complex applications where the access patterns vary or depend on user input.

Timeouts are also used as a pragmatic form of deadlock handling. Instead of waiting indefinitely for a lock, a transaction is configured to wait for a maximum amount of time. If the lock is not granted within that window, the transaction assumes that a deadlock or severe contention is occurring and aborts itself. While this approach does not prevent deadlocks, it provides a mechanism to escape from them without requiring explicit cycle detection. It is particularly useful in distributed systems or databases with long-running queries, where waiting indefinitely would consume valuable resources and reduce throughput.

Database administrators can take proactive steps to reduce the frequency and impact of deadlocks. One key practice is keeping transactions short and focused. The longer a transaction holds locks, the greater the window of opportunity for deadlocks to occur. Breaking large operations into smaller, discrete transactions not only minimizes lock duration but also reduces contention across shared resources. Another important strategy is indexing, which can significantly reduce the number of rows scanned and locked during query execution. By improving query performance and reducing the amount of data touched by each transaction, indexes indirectly reduce the likelihood of deadlocks.

Monitoring tools also play a crucial role in identifying and diagnosing deadlocks. Most database systems provide logs or dynamic views that record deadlock events, including the transactions involved, the resources they were waiting on, and the queries that led to the conflict. By analyzing this information, administrators can pinpoint problematic code paths or transaction patterns and take corrective action. This might involve rewriting queries, adding indexes, or redesigning application logic to access data in a more predictable and lock-friendly manner.

Advanced databases may implement techniques such as lock-free or latch-free data structures and multiversion concurrency control to further reduce locking and eliminate many types of deadlocks entirely. These approaches allow multiple versions of data to coexist, enabling readers and writers to operate in parallel without acquiring conflicting locks. While these models are powerful and reduce contention, they introduce their own complexities in terms of storage management and transaction validation. Nevertheless, for high-concurrency environments, these systems provide an attractive alternative to traditional locking mechanisms.

In the end, deadlocks are an inevitable reality in any system where transactions access shared resources concurrently. They are not failures of the database but a natural outcome of complex interdependencies between operations. What distinguishes robust systems from fragile ones is how well they detect, resolve, and recover from deadlocks. Developers and administrators must work together to write resilient applications, optimize transaction logic, and monitor system behavior. By doing so, they can ensure that deadlocks, while occasionally unavoidable, do not undermine the performance, stability, or reliability of the database system.

Replication Strategies and Indexing Impact

Replication is a key technique in modern database systems that enhances availability, scalability, and fault tolerance by maintaining copies of data across multiple servers. It enables systems to continue functioning in the event of hardware failure, support geographic distribution of data, and balance read workloads by directing queries to replica servers. However, the strategy chosen for replication can significantly affect system behavior, particularly in relation to indexing. Indexes, which are vital for efficient data retrieval, must be carefully considered in replicated environments because they can influence replication performance, consistency, storage requirements, and query optimization in both the primary and secondary databases. Understanding how replication and indexing interact is critical for designing systems that perform reliably under various loads and failover scenarios.

There are several primary replication strategies used in relational databases: synchronous replication, asynchronous replication, and semi-synchronous replication. Each of these approaches presents different trade-offs between consistency, latency, and fault tolerance. In synchronous replication, every change made on the primary database is immediately applied to all replicas before the transaction is considered committed. This ensures strong consistency across nodes but can introduce significant latency, particularly if replicas are geographically distant. Asynchronous replication allows the primary to commit changes without waiting for replicas, which improves performance but risks temporary data inconsistency if a failure occurs before replication completes. Semi-synchronous replication strikes a balance by waiting for at least one replica to acknowledge receipt before committing the transaction.

The indexing strategy used on the primary server can influence replication in both direct and indirect ways. Indexes affect the speed of writes, which in turn affects replication lag in asynchronous systems. Every insert, update, or delete operation requires corresponding changes to all relevant indexes. The more indexes a table has, and the more complex those indexes are, the longer write operations take. In an asynchronous replication setup, this can lead to increased delay between the primary and the replicas, especially under write-heavy workloads. If replication cannot keep up with the rate of change, replicas will lag behind, which may affect applications relying on near-real-time data access from those replicas.

On the replica side, the presence or absence of indexes can dramatically alter the utility and performance of the replica. In some systems, particularly read-only replicas, it may be desirable to define different indexes than those used on the primary server. These custom indexes can be optimized for the specific read workloads served by the replica, such as reporting queries or analytics, which may have different access patterns than the transactional queries on the primary. For example, the primary might prioritize indexes that support fast inserts and updates, while the replica might include indexes that speed up aggregations or full-table scans. However, introducing too many indexes on the replica can increase the time required to apply replicated changes, potentially causing replication lag even if the replica is read-only.

The mechanism of replication itself also affects how indexes are maintained. In statement-based replication, SQL statements executed on the primary are replayed on the replica. This approach requires the same schema and indexes on all nodes to ensure consistency, as different indexing structures could lead to different execution plans and non-deterministic behavior. Row-based replication, by contrast, transfers the actual data changes (such as row images) rather than SQL statements, allowing for some variation in schema or indexing on the replicas. This flexibility can be leveraged to tailor indexing strategies on replicas without compromising data consistency. However, it introduces additional storage and processing overhead to capture and transmit row-level changes.

Conflict resolution is another area where indexing can play a role, particularly in multi-master or active-active replication setups. In these environments, where multiple nodes can accept write operations, conflicts can occur when the same piece of data is modified on more than one node simultaneously. Efficient detection and resolution of these conflicts often rely on indexes to identify conflicting rows and apply resolution rules quickly. If indexes are missing or poorly designed, conflict resolution can become slow or error-prone, undermining the reliability of the replication strategy.

Monitoring replication performance is essential, and indexing decisions should be guided by observed replication metrics such as transaction commit latency, replication lag, and throughput. Indexes should be evaluated not only for their impact on query performance but also for their role in the replication process. In highly dynamic environments, it may be necessary to adjust indexing strategies over time as replication patterns evolve or as the read/write workload distribution shifts between the primary and replicas.

Replication strategies also intersect with indexing in terms of recovery and failover. In a failover scenario, a replica is promoted to become the new primary. If the indexing on the replica is not aligned with the needs of a primary workload, performance can suffer post-failover. To mitigate this, some systems ensure that all replicas maintain a set of core indexes necessary for write operations, even if those indexes are not used during normal read-only operation. This dual-purpose indexing ensures a smoother transition during failover events and minimizes the risk of performance degradation at critical moments.

In cloud and distributed databases, replication and indexing must account for network latency, partition tolerance, and elasticity. Systems like distributed SQL databases replicate data across regions or availability zones to provide high availability and disaster recovery. In these setups, indexing strategies must be carefully balanced to avoid excessive resource usage and to support diverse query patterns from distributed applications. Index rebuilds, for instance, can trigger large volumes of replicated changes if not coordinated properly, leading to spikes in replication traffic and potential instability.

Ultimately, replication strategies are not isolated decisions but are deeply entwined with the broader system architecture, including how indexes are created, maintained, and used. Designing an indexing strategy that complements the replication approach requires a comprehensive understanding of workload characteristics, replication topology, and consistency requirements. By considering the impact of indexing on both replication efficiency and read performance across all nodes, database architects can create systems that not only remain consistent and available but also deliver high-speed access to data, regardless of where or how it is consumed.

Partitioning Data for Performance

Partitioning data is a powerful strategy in database design that significantly enhances performance, scalability, and manageability, especially in systems dealing with large volumes of information. The central idea behind partitioning is to divide a large dataset into smaller, more manageable segments called partitions. Each partition is stored and managed independently, but together they form a complete logical table. This segmentation allows queries and operations to target only the relevant partitions instead of scanning the entire table, which reduces I/O, speeds up response time, and makes maintenance tasks more efficient. When implemented correctly, partitioning becomes a vital technique for high-performance database systems, particularly in data warehouses, analytical platforms, and large transactional systems.

There are several partitioning methods, each suited for different data distribution and access patterns. Range partitioning divides data based on a range of values in a specific column. For example, a sales table could be partitioned by year, so all records for 2020 go into one partition, 2021 into another, and so on. This type of partitioning is especially effective for time-series data, where queries often target recent periods. Hash partitioning uses a hashing algorithm to distribute rows evenly across partitions based on the value of a specific column, such as customer ID. This approach is beneficial when access patterns are unpredictable and ensures uniform data distribution, which prevents hotspots and balances load. List partitioning assigns rows to partitions based on specific, discrete values of a column. Composite partitioning combines multiple methods, such as range and hash, to leverage the strengths of both approaches.

One of the main performance benefits of partitioning is partition pruning. When a query includes a filter on the partitioning column, the database engine can eliminate irrelevant partitions from the scan, reducing the amount of data read and processed. For example, a query retrieving orders from January 2022 in a range-partitioned table by month only scans the January 2022 partition instead of the entire orders table. This selective scanning dramatically improves query speed and reduces resource consumption. Partition pruning is automatic in most database systems, provided that queries are written to include the partitioning column in the WHERE clause. Developers and administrators must understand how their database handles pruning to ensure that partitioning delivers its full performance benefits.

Partitioning also enhances performance by enabling parallelism. Since partitions are stored and accessed independently, many database engines can process them in parallel across multiple CPU cores or nodes. This capability is particularly useful for large analytical queries that scan or aggregate vast amounts of data. Each partition can be read and processed independently, and the partial results can be combined at the end, leveraging modern hardware to reduce query execution time. This parallelism extends to maintenance operations as well. Index rebuilding, data loading, and backup tasks can be executed at the partition level, making them faster and less disruptive to the overall system.

Indexing in partitioned tables introduces unique considerations. Indexes can be either global or local. Global indexes span the entire table and are unaware of partition boundaries. Local indexes, on the other hand, are created and maintained independently for each partition. Local indexes align with the partitioning strategy and are easier to manage because they can be rebuilt or dropped at the partition level. They also benefit from partition pruning, as queries that target a specific partition will use the corresponding local index without scanning irrelevant index segments. However, local indexes may not perform well for queries that join partitioned and non-partitioned tables unless designed carefully. Global indexes offer better performance for some cross-partition queries but can be more expensive to maintain, especially when partitions are added or removed.

Partitioning also improves data lifecycle management. In systems where data ages and becomes less frequently accessed, partitions allow old data to be archived or purged efficiently. Dropping a partition is much faster than deleting millions of rows from a table, and it avoids generating large amounts of undo and redo logs. This approach is common in financial and telecommunications systems where data retention policies require historical data to be kept for years but rarely queried. By organizing data into partitions based on time or activity, administrators can easily isolate and remove old partitions without affecting current operations.

Despite its advantages, partitioning introduces complexity in schema design and query optimization. Choosing the right partitioning key is crucial. A poor choice can result in uneven data distribution, which leads to some partitions being much larger or more active than others, creating bottlenecks. For example, partitioning a table by region might seem logical, but if most transactions happen in just one or two regions, those partitions will become hotspots, negating the benefits of partitioning. Similarly, hash partitioning can distribute data evenly but may not support partition pruning if queries do not include the partitioning column. Therefore, understanding data access patterns and workload characteristics is essential when designing a partitioning strategy.

Partitioning also interacts with replication and high availability strategies. In distributed databases, partitions may be spread across multiple nodes, with each node responsible for a subset of the data. This distribution supports horizontal scaling and ensures that no single node becomes a bottleneck. However, it also requires careful coordination to maintain consistency and to route queries to the correct node. Some systems use partition-aware query planners or routers that direct requests based on the partitioning logic. Failover and recovery processes must also account for the location and state of partitions to avoid data loss or unavailability.

Testing and monitoring are critical when implementing partitioning. Queries should be tested to verify that partition pruning is effective and that performance gains are realized. Execution plans should be reviewed regularly to ensure that indexes and partitioning strategies continue to align with evolving access patterns. As the system grows, the partitioning scheme may need to be adjusted, either by redefining the boundaries or by implementing sub-partitioning. Partitioning should not be viewed as a one-time decision but as an adaptable strategy that evolves with the application's data and usage.

Partitioning data for performance is a strategic investment in the scalability and maintainability of database systems. It allows organizations to handle larger datasets, accelerate query performance, and manage data growth more effectively. By aligning partitioning strategies with access patterns, indexing schemes, and system architecture, database professionals can unlock significant performance improvements and build systems that remain efficient and responsive under increasing loads.

Sharding Considerations in Distributed Databases

Sharding is a technique used in distributed database systems to handle massive volumes of data by dividing it into smaller, more manageable pieces called shards. Each shard represents a subset of the total dataset and is typically stored on a separate server or node within a distributed infrastructure. The primary goal of sharding is to achieve horizontal scalability, allowing a database to support increasing loads by simply adding more nodes. However, implementing sharding is not a trivial task. It requires careful planning, deep understanding of the application's data access patterns, and an awareness of the implications for performance, consistency, availability, and maintenance. The decisions made during the design and implementation of a sharding strategy can have long-lasting effects on how the system performs and evolves.

The first consideration in a sharded architecture is the choice of shard key. This key determines how data is distributed across the shards. An ideal shard key evenly distributes data and load, minimizing hotspots and ensuring that no single node becomes a bottleneck. A poorly chosen shard key can lead to uneven distribution, where some shards store significantly more data or receive more queries than others, defeating the purpose of sharding. For example, using a country code as a shard key may lead to imbalanced load if a majority of users come from just a few countries. Similarly, choosing a monotonically increasing key such as an auto-incremented ID can cause new data to be written to the same shard repeatedly, creating write hotspots and overwhelming a single node.

Once the shard key is selected, the system must determine the sharding method. Common approaches include range-based sharding, hash-based sharding, and directory-based sharding. Range-based sharding assigns data to shards based on contiguous ranges of the shard key. This is intuitive and supports range queries efficiently but risks imbalance if the key distribution is skewed. Hash-based sharding applies a hash function to the shard key, distributing records more uniformly across nodes. While this approach mitigates hotspots, it makes range queries more complex and often requires data aggregation across multiple shards. Directory-based sharding maintains a lookup table that maps each record or entity to a specific shard. Although flexible, this method introduces an additional layer of complexity and potential single points of failure.

Query routing is another crucial aspect of sharding. In a sharded database, the system must determine which shard contains the data needed to satisfy a query. If the query includes the shard key, routing is straightforward and efficient. However, if the shard key is not part of the query condition, the system may need to broadcast the query to all shards, significantly increasing latency and resource consumption. This phenomenon, known as a scatter-gather operation, is one of the primary performance concerns in sharded systems. It can degrade performance and overwhelm network and compute resources, particularly in systems with a large number of shards. Therefore, application developers must be trained to write queries that are shard-aware and include the shard key whenever possible.

Sharding also impacts transaction management and consistency. In a non-sharded system, the database engine can easily enforce ACID properties across all data. In a sharded environment, maintaining consistency across shards becomes more challenging, especially for transactions that span multiple shards. These cross-shard transactions require coordination between nodes and often rely on distributed consensus protocols or two-phase commit mechanisms. These protocols introduce latency and increase the likelihood of failure due to the higher number of participating nodes. To mitigate this, many distributed databases encourage designs that localize transactions to a single shard. This often requires denormalizing data or restructuring the schema to keep related data together within the same shard.

Backup and recovery operations are more complex in a sharded environment. Each shard must be backed up independently, and consistency across shards must be maintained to ensure a reliable system snapshot. During recovery, all shards must be restored to a consistent point in time to avoid logical corruption or data loss. This requires careful coordination, especially in systems that replicate data across regions or maintain different consistency levels for different shards. The use of logical clocks, write-ahead logs, or version vectors can help align shards during recovery, but they add complexity to system design and maintenance.

Resharding is another critical consideration. Over time, data distribution and access patterns may change, making the original shard configuration suboptimal. Rebalancing shards or changing the shard key becomes necessary to maintain performance and prevent overload on specific nodes. Resharding is a complex and often disruptive process that involves redistributing large volumes of data while keeping the system online and consistent. It requires sophisticated data migration tools, careful orchestration, and monitoring to avoid downtime or data inconsistencies. Some modern distributed databases provide automated resharding features, but these capabilities are not universally available and often come with trade-offs in terms of control and visibility.

High availability and fault tolerance must also be addressed in a sharded system. Since each shard typically resides on a different node, the failure of one node affects only a subset of the data. This architecture improves fault isolation, but it also means that availability depends on the ability to recover or failover individual shards. Implementing replication within each shard ensures that data is not lost if a node fails. Failover mechanisms must be able to promote replica nodes quickly and reroute traffic with minimal disruption. In some systems, replication and sharding are tightly integrated, allowing seamless recovery, while in others, they must be configured and managed separately.

Monitoring and observability in a sharded environment require a different approach than in traditional monolithic databases. Administrators must track metrics across all shards, such as query latency, replication lag, disk usage, and resource contention. Centralized dashboards and alerting systems help manage this complexity, but they must scale to handle the volume of data generated by multiple nodes. Without proper observability, diagnosing performance issues or failures becomes difficult, and small problems can escalate unnoticed. Logging must also be sharded-aware to correlate events across the distributed system.

Security and access control become more nuanced in sharded databases. Ensuring that permissions, encryption, and audit policies are consistently applied across all shards requires centralized management or automation. In multi-tenant architectures, sharding is often used to isolate tenants, but this must be complemented with strict security policies to prevent cross-tenant access or data leaks. Encryption at rest and in transit should be enforced consistently, and key management must scale with the number of shards.

Sharding enables distributed databases to scale horizontally and support high volumes of data and traffic. However, it comes with complexity in design, implementation, and operation. Choosing the right shard key, designing for query routing, handling cross-shard transactions, planning for resharding, and maintaining observability are all essential to building a robust and efficient sharded architecture. When done well, sharding empowers applications to deliver consistent, high-performance experiences at scale, even in the face of growing demand and evolving workloads.

Using Materialized Views for Speed

Materialized views are a powerful performance optimization feature in relational database systems, especially useful in scenarios where queries involve complex joins, aggregations, or computations over large datasets. Unlike regular views, which are virtual and evaluated on the fly every time they are accessed, materialized views store the actual results of a query physically on disk. This persistent storage means that subsequent queries against the materialized view can be answered much more quickly, since the database does not need to reprocess the underlying tables each time. Materialized views are particularly valuable in analytical workloads, reporting systems, and data warehouses, where performance and query response times are critical and where data changes less frequently.

The key advantage of using materialized views lies in their ability to precompute and store expensive query results. For example, consider a reporting dashboard that displays daily sales totals, average order values, and customer counts across multiple regions. Without materialized views, each metric might require multiple joins and aggregations over large fact tables, causing high CPU and I/O usage. By creating a materialized view that already contains these metrics pre-aggregated by day and region, the system can respond to dashboard requests in milliseconds instead of minutes. This allows users to explore data interactively without putting strain on the primary database tables.

Materialized views are defined using a standard SELECT statement that specifies which columns, tables, and filters should be included in the view. Once created, the database engine executes the query and stores the result as a physical table. Indexes can be added to this table just like any other, further enhancing query performance. Some databases also support automatic query rewriting, where the optimizer transparently redirects a user query to the materialized view if it can satisfy the request more efficiently than querying the base tables. This rewriting process depends on the view definition and the query structure being compatible, and it enables performance benefits without requiring changes to the application or user queries.

One of the most important design decisions when working with materialized views is determining how and when the view should be refreshed. Since the data in a materialized view is a snapshot of the data at the time of its last refresh, it can become stale if the underlying tables are frequently updated. Most systems support two primary refresh modes: complete and incremental. A complete refresh recomputes the entire view from scratch, replacing the previous contents with the new results. This approach is straightforward but can be time-consuming for large views. An incremental, or fast refresh, updates only the changes since the last refresh by using logs or triggers to capture modifications. This method is more efficient but requires the underlying tables to be structured in a way that supports change tracking.

The frequency of refreshing a materialized view depends on the use case. In some reporting systems, it is acceptable for the data to be refreshed hourly or nightly, particularly if the reports are used for strategic decisions and not for real-time operations. In other applications, such as real-time monitoring or operational dashboards, near-instantaneous updates may be required. Some databases allow materialized views to be refreshed automatically at defined intervals or even immediately after underlying data changes. However, real-time refresh capabilities typically introduce overhead on insert, update, and delete operations, so the trade-off between data freshness and write performance must be carefully evaluated.

Materialized views also provide benefits beyond performance. They can simplify application logic by encapsulating complex queries in a reusable structure. Instead of embedding the same lengthy join and aggregation logic in multiple queries or applications, developers can reference the materialized view as a single object. This improves maintainability, reduces the chance of errors, and makes it easier to adapt to changes in business requirements. When the view definition needs to be updated, only the materialized view itself needs to be modified, rather than changing all dependent queries.

Despite their benefits, materialized views must be used judiciously. They consume additional storage since they duplicate data from base tables. Depending on the number and complexity of views, this overhead can become significant. Furthermore, maintaining materialized views introduces extra workload during data modification operations. In systems with frequent updates or large batch loads, the cost of refreshing views must be weighed against the performance gains for read operations. Monitoring the performance impact and usage frequency of each view helps ensure that resources are being used effectively.

Indexing materialized views is another performance consideration. Because these views are physical structures, they can be indexed just like regular tables. Adding indexes on commonly queried columns in the materialized view can further reduce query response times. However, each index also adds overhead during refresh operations. Therefore, indexes should be chosen based on actual query patterns, and unused indexes should be periodically reviewed and dropped. In some systems, clustered indexes or partitioning can be applied to materialized views, allowing even greater control over performance optimization.

In distributed or replicated database environments, materialized views offer a mechanism for local caching of remote data. For example, a branch office might maintain a materialized view of central warehouse inventory to speed up local queries and reduce dependency on the network. These local views can be refreshed periodically to stay in sync with the central system. This technique reduces latency and improves fault tolerance in geographically dispersed systems. However, it also introduces consistency challenges, especially if the underlying data changes frequently and the views are not refreshed in real time.

Security and access control must also be considered when using materialized views. Because these views store actual data, access to them must be governed by the same rules and restrictions as the base tables. In some systems, materialized views are used to expose subsets of sensitive data to specific users or applications. For instance, a view might include aggregated sales data by region but omit customer-level details, allowing safe access to summary information without exposing individual records. This approach provides both performance and data protection benefits.

Materialized views are a versatile and effective tool for improving database performance, especially in scenarios involving large datasets and complex queries. By storing the results of expensive operations in a persistent structure and refreshing them strategically, they enable faster query response times, reduced resource usage, and more scalable applications. As with any optimization technique, the key to successful use lies in thoughtful design, regular monitoring, and continuous alignment with evolving data and workload patterns. When used appropriately, materialized views can significantly enhance the responsiveness and efficiency of database systems, providing real value to both developers and end users.

Backup Fundamentals and Types

Backups are a cornerstone of database administration, ensuring that data can be recovered in the event of failure, corruption, accidental deletion, or disaster. A backup is essentially a copy of data taken at a specific point in time and stored in a secure location, allowing recovery to that point should the need arise. While the concept may seem straightforward, the implementation of effective backup strategies is far more complex, involving careful consideration of performance, storage, recovery time objectives, and system availability. Backups are not only about making copies but about creating a robust safety net that guarantees business continuity and protects against data loss in any circumstance.

One of the most fundamental decisions in backup planning is determining what type of backup to perform. There are three primary types: full, differential, and incremental. A full backup captures the entire dataset, including all databases, tables, and metadata at the time of the backup. This type of backup provides a complete snapshot of the system and is the foundation upon which other backup types are built. Full backups are the most reliable and simplest to restore but also the most time-consuming and storage-intensive. Due to their size, they are typically scheduled less frequently and supplemented by other backup types to minimize system impact.

Differential backups are based on the most recent full backup. They capture only the changes made since that full backup, regardless of how many differential backups have been taken in the meantime. This method reduces the amount of data backed up and the time required compared to full backups, while still providing a comprehensive recovery point. When restoring from a differential backup, both the last full backup and the most recent differential backup are required. This strikes a balance between restore time and backup efficiency, making differential backups a popular choice in environments where data changes frequently but fast recovery is also a priority.

Incremental backups take the idea of optimization even further. Unlike differential backups, which always include all changes since the last full backup, incremental backups only include changes made since the last backup of any type, whether full or incremental. This results in very small and quick backup files, especially in systems with minimal daily changes. However, restoring from incremental backups is more complex because it requires the last full backup plus every subsequent incremental backup up to the desired point in time. The restore process must replay each incremental backup in sequence, which can be time-consuming. Nevertheless, incremental backups are ideal for systems with limited bandwidth, storage constraints, or when frequent backups are needed throughout the day.

Another important backup concept is the distinction between logical and physical backups. Logical backups extract data in a human-readable format such as SQL dump files, which can be re-imported to recreate the database. These backups are portable and easy to inspect or modify but can be slower to restore, especially for large datasets. Physical backups, on the other hand, involve copying the actual database files, including data files, transaction logs, and configuration files. This method is typically faster to restore and maintains exact system state, making it suitable for disaster recovery and high-performance applications. Physical backups are often tied to the specific database engine and environment in which they were created.

Modern backup strategies often incorporate additional layers of protection, such as transaction log backups and snapshot technologies. Transaction log backups allow point-in-time recovery by capturing a record of all changes made to the database since the last backup. This is particularly valuable in high-availability environments where losing even a few minutes of data is unacceptable. By combining a full backup, differential or incremental backups, and transaction log backups, administrators can recreate the database at virtually any moment, down to the second, depending on the granularity of log capture.

Snapshots, typically used in storage-level backups, create a read-only copy of the database's state at a specific moment without actually copying data. Instead, they rely on copy-on-write mechanisms to preserve the original data while allowing changes to continue in the live system. Snapshots are fast and efficient but are best suited for short-term protection or as part of a broader backup plan. They are also highly dependent on the underlying storage system and may not provide sufficient resilience on their own without being combined with full or incremental backups stored in independent locations.

Backup frequency and retention policies are another core element of backup strategy. The backup schedule must align with the organization's recovery time objective (RTO) and recovery point objective (RPO). RTO defines how quickly a system must be restored after a failure, while RPO defines how much data loss is acceptable. For example, a critical financial system may have an RTO of one hour and an RPO of zero, meaning it must be back online within an hour and no data can be lost. Meeting these objectives may require hourly transaction log backups, daily full backups, and weekly offsite backups, with a retention period of several months or even years depending on regulatory requirements.

Storage location and redundancy are also critical factors. Storing backups on the same physical server or network as the primary data exposes the system to risks such as hardware failure, ransomware, or site-wide disasters. Best practices dictate storing backups in multiple, geographically dispersed locations, including offline or immutable storage solutions that cannot be modified or deleted by malicious actors. Cloud-based storage offers flexibility, scalability, and durability, but it must be balanced against costs, data sovereignty regulations, and access latency. Hybrid approaches that combine local and cloud backups provide fast recovery for recent backups and long-term protection against catastrophic events.

Automation and monitoring are essential for effective backup management. Backup processes should be automated to run at scheduled intervals without manual intervention, with thorough logging and alerting in place to detect and report failures. Simply assuming a backup job completed successfully is a dangerous mistake. Regular testing of backup integrity and restoration procedures is equally important. A backup that cannot be restored is effectively worthless. Organizations must periodically perform test restores to verify that data can be recovered as expected, and that documentation, scripts, and procedures are accurate and up to date.

Backups are not just a technical task but a business-critical process that supports compliance, continuity, and trust. Regulations in industries such as finance, healthcare, and government often mandate specific backup and retention policies. Non-compliance can result in legal penalties, reputational damage, and financial loss. Therefore, backup strategies must be clearly defined, documented, and integrated into broader disaster recovery and business continuity plans. All stakeholders, including IT, security, and business leadership, should understand their roles and responsibilities in maintaining a resilient data environment.

Understanding backup fundamentals and implementing the appropriate types of backups ensures that organizations are prepared for any eventuality. Whether recovering from an accidental deletion, a failed upgrade, or a full system crash, a well-planned backup system enables quick, reliable recovery with minimal disruption. In an increasingly data-driven world, the ability to restore lost or corrupted data quickly and accurately is not just an operational necessity but a foundational element of trust in digital systems.

Hot vs Cold Backup Techniques

Backup techniques in relational database systems are classified based on whether the database remains online and accessible during the backup process. The two primary approaches are known as hot backups and cold backups. Each method serves distinct operational needs and introduces unique trade-offs in terms of availability, complexity, speed, and risk. Selecting between hot and cold backups, or deciding to implement both as part of a layered backup strategy, depends heavily on the business requirements for uptime, the nature of the workload, and the technology stack used to host the database.

A hot backup, also referred to as an online backup, is performed while the database remains operational and accessible to users and applications. This method is essential in environments that require high availability and cannot afford downtime. During a hot backup, the database engine continues to process reads and writes, while simultaneously creating a consistent snapshot of the data at a specific point in time. This process is made possible through coordination with internal mechanisms such as transaction logs, redo logs, and temporary locks. Hot backups are designed to capture a recoverable state without interrupting business operations, making them ideal for systems that operate around the clock, such as e-commerce platforms, banking applications, and critical healthcare systems.

To maintain consistency during a hot backup, the database engine ensures that all changes made during the backup window are tracked and can be reapplied later if needed. This is often achieved using write-ahead logging, which captures all modifications before they are written to the data files. When restoring a hot backup, these logs are replayed to bring the database to a consistent state, as of the exact moment the backup completed. This level of detail supports point-in-time recovery and offers robust protection against both hardware failure and human error. However, hot backups can impact performance during the backup window due to the additional I/O and resource consumption required to track changes and copy data concurrently.

Cold backups, in contrast, are performed when the database is shut down and no transactions are being processed. This approach ensures that all files are in a consistent state, eliminating the need for transaction logs to replay or reconcile changes. Because the system is inactive during the backup, there is no risk of partial transactions or concurrent writes compromising the integrity of the backup. Cold backups are often used in smaller systems or environments where downtime during non-peak hours is acceptable. For example, an internal HR database might be backed up nightly using a cold backup while the system is offline.

Cold backups are generally simpler to perform and restore because they involve copying the physical files as-is, without worrying about in-flight transactions or active connections. The reduced complexity can lead to faster and more reliable restores, especially in situations where transaction log replay is not necessary or practical. However, the obvious disadvantage is that the database must be taken offline, which can be a significant disruption in environments with high availability requirements. In modern, globalized applications with users operating in multiple time zones, even short maintenance windows can be difficult to schedule.

The choice between hot and cold backup techniques often hinges on the recovery time objective and recovery point objective of the organization. Hot backups, by supporting frequent and non-disruptive operations, enable tighter RPOs and shorter RTOs, especially when combined with incremental backups or continuous log archiving. Cold backups, while potentially offering faster restore times for small datasets, often lead to longer RPOs, as data changes between backups cannot be captured unless complemented by additional backup types such as transaction log backups.

Database engines offer specific tools and commands to support both hot and cold backups. In Oracle, for example, hot backups require the database to be in ARCHIVELOG mode, allowing the system to track and archive changes during the backup process. Cold backups, by contrast, are performed by simply stopping the database and copying the data, control, and log files using operating system tools. PostgreSQL supports hot backups via streaming replication and base backups using the pg_basebackup utility, while cold backups involve stopping the PostgreSQL server and archiving the entire data directory.

Advanced implementations sometimes combine both techniques in hybrid strategies. For instance, a full cold backup might be performed weekly, with daily hot backups or continuous archiving supplementing it during the week. This layered approach provides multiple recovery points and balances performance impact with operational resilience. In high-compliance industries, such as finance or healthcare, regulations may dictate the use of hot backups to ensure minimal data loss, while also requiring periodic cold backups for archival purposes and long-term storage in offsite or immutable systems.

Security and access control are also important when managing both hot and cold backups. Because backups often contain sensitive data, they must be encrypted during both transport and storage. Hot backups, which are frequently streamed to remote storage systems, require secure channels such as TLS or VPNs. Cold backups, often stored on physical media or offline storage devices, must be protected against unauthorized access, loss, or tampering. Role-based access controls, audit logs, and regular verification checks are essential to ensure that backups remain both confidential and usable when needed.

Monitoring and automation are crucial in both hot and cold backup strategies. Automated tools can schedule backup jobs, verify integrity, compress files, and alert administrators to failures or anomalies. For hot backups, monitoring tools must track performance metrics to ensure that the backup process does not interfere with live operations. For cold backups, alerts about failed shutdowns, incomplete copies, or disk errors can prevent disasters before they occur. In all cases, backups must be regularly tested by performing real restores in a controlled environment to confirm that the process works and the data is intact.

Storage planning is another critical aspect. Hot backups typically produce large files that must be stored quickly and efficiently, often in real time. This necessitates the use of high-speed disks, scalable cloud storage, or deduplication solutions. Cold backups, while often created during low-usage periods, still require careful storage management, especially for systems with large volumes or regulatory retention requirements. Proper labeling, versioning, and documentation ensure that the right backup is restored in an emergency, avoiding confusion and costly delays.

Ultimately, both hot and cold backup techniques serve vital roles in a comprehensive data protection strategy. Each has strengths and limitations, and neither is universally superior. The optimal approach depends on the operational environment, data volatility, user expectations, compliance requirements, and technical capabilities of the organization. By understanding the mechanisms and implications of each method, database professionals can build resilient systems that maintain data integrity and availability under any conditions.

Point-In-Time Recovery

Point-in-time recovery is a powerful feature in relational database systems that allows administrators to restore a database to a specific moment in the past, down to the exact second. This capability is essential in environments where data accuracy and continuity are critical, and where the potential for human error, application bugs, or malicious activity poses a constant threat. Whether it is the result of an accidental deletion, a corrupted batch update, or a ransomware attack, point-in-time recovery enables organizations to minimize data loss by precisely targeting the moment just before the damaging event occurred. Unlike full or differential backups that restore the database to the state it was in at the time the backup was taken, point-in-time recovery bridges the gap between backups by applying transaction logs or archived redo logs to incrementally roll the database forward to the desired recovery point.

At the core of point-in-time recovery is the concept of log-based restoration. Most relational databases use transaction logs to record every change made to the data. These logs serve two critical purposes: they provide durability by ensuring that committed changes can survive crashes, and they offer a mechanism for replaying changes to recreate a historical state. To perform a point-in-time recovery, the process begins with restoring a full backup of the database to a temporary or recovery instance. Once the base data is in place, the system replays the transaction logs, applying each change in the exact order it occurred, until it reaches the designated recovery point. At this moment, the process stops, and the database is brought online in the same logical state it was in at the target time.

Implementing point-in-time recovery requires careful planning and precise configuration. The database must be set up to archive transaction logs continuously and to retain them for a period sufficient to support recovery within the organization's recovery point objective. If transaction logs are missing or corrupted, the recovery can only proceed up to the last available log, potentially leading to unacceptable data loss. This makes the consistent archiving and monitoring of logs a critical component of any point-in-time recovery strategy. Storage systems must be reliable and redundant, and administrators must regularly verify the presence and integrity of archived logs to ensure that they are usable when needed.

The accuracy of point-in-time recovery also depends on the granularity of timekeeping within the database system. Some databases allow recovery to be specified using timestamps, transaction identifiers, or log sequence numbers. The choice of recovery marker affects the precision and usability of the process. Timestamps are human-readable and easy to reference, making them ideal for recovering from events tied to known real-world actions. However, they can be affected by system clock drift or synchronization issues. Log sequence numbers, while more technical, offer exact positioning within the transaction stream, ensuring that recovery occurs at the precise point in the log where the issue began.

One of the most common use cases for point-in-time recovery is undoing accidental operations. For example, a developer might run a DELETE statement without a WHERE clause, removing all rows from a critical table. If the mistake is detected quickly, the administrator can perform a point-in-time recovery to the second before the command was issued, restoring the table without losing subsequent changes in other areas. This form of targeted correction is far more efficient and less disruptive than restoring the entire system from a backup. It also reduces the recovery time objective, allowing businesses to resume normal operations much faster than traditional recovery methods.

Point-in-time recovery can be implemented at the database, schema, or table level, depending on the capabilities of the system. Some databases, such as PostgreSQL, support whole-database point-in-time recovery but do not allow recovery of individual tables unless additional tools or logical replication is used. Other platforms, like Oracle, offer more granular recovery options, allowing administrators to recover a single table or partition without affecting the rest of the system. The choice of recovery scope has implications for downtime and complexity, and it must be aligned with the organization's recovery time objectives and operational constraints.

To perform point-in-time recovery safely, many administrators use a staging or recovery server. This separate environment allows the recovery to be completed without disrupting the production system. Once the recovery reaches the target time, the relevant data can be extracted and reintegrated into the live database using export and import tools, replication, or custom scripts. This approach provides maximum control over the recovery process and minimizes the risk of further damage during restoration. It also supports verification and testing, ensuring that the recovered data is accurate and complete before it is reintroduced into production.

Automation and scripting play a vital role in successful point-in-time recovery. In high-volume systems with frequent transactions, manually identifying the exact recovery point and applying logs can be error-prone and time-consuming. Automation tools can track transaction logs, correlate them with application activity, and generate scripts to perform the restore and replay steps in a controlled and repeatable manner. These tools also help enforce retention policies, ensure that archived logs are properly stored and cataloged, and monitor for anomalies that could indicate failed backups or missing logs.

Point-in-time recovery is not just a technical safeguard but a business enabler. It provides peace of mind to application developers and operations teams, knowing that mistakes can be corrected without catastrophic consequences. It also supports compliance and audit requirements by enabling data recovery in response to unauthorized changes or policy violations. In sectors such as finance, healthcare, and legal services, where data integrity is paramount and data loss can result in severe regulatory penalties, the ability to restore data to a known good state at a precise moment is a critical capability.

However, the success of point-in-time recovery depends entirely on the preparedness of the organization. Without properly configured logging, reliable backups, and a tested recovery plan, the theoretical ability to recover to a specific point is meaningless. Database teams must regularly simulate recovery scenarios, validate that backups are complete and recoverable, and maintain detailed documentation of recovery procedures. Recovery drills help build confidence, uncover hidden dependencies, and ensure that the entire team can respond quickly and effectively when an actual recovery is required.

Point-in-time recovery transforms how organizations handle data integrity challenges, offering flexibility, control, and precision in recovering from unplanned incidents. By integrating this capability into the overall data protection strategy, businesses gain resilience against the unpredictable, whether it is human error, application failure, or malicious interference. The ability to turn back the clock, precisely and reliably, is one of the most powerful tools available in the realm of database administration.

Incremental and Differential Backups

Incremental and differential backups are essential components of modern database backup strategies, designed to optimize storage usage, reduce backup windows, and support more granular recovery options. While full backups remain the foundation of any backup plan, they are often too large and time-consuming to perform frequently in environments with high data volumes or 24/7 availability requirements. To overcome these limitations, incremental and differential backups are employed to capture only the data that has changed since a previous reference point, significantly reducing the time and resources needed for each backup operation. The primary difference between the two lies in what they consider as their baseline and how much data they include with each backup iteration.

An incremental backup captures only the data that has changed since the most recent backup, whether that backup was full or incremental. This means that after the initial full backup, each subsequent incremental backup is small and quick, containing only the newly modified data blocks or files. Because each backup contains the minimum possible amount of data, this method is highly efficient in terms of both storage and bandwidth. However, this efficiency comes with complexity during recovery. To restore the database to a specific point, the recovery process must begin with the last full backup and apply every incremental backup in sequence, up to the desired moment. If any one of the incremental files is missing or corrupted, the entire chain is broken, and recovery may fail or be incomplete.

In contrast, a differential backup captures all changes made since the last full backup, regardless of how many differential backups have been performed in between. Each differential backup includes the cumulative set of changes, growing in size over time until the next full backup is taken. This results in larger backup files compared to incremental backups, especially when the interval between full backups is long. However, differential backups offer faster and simpler recovery than incremental backups because only the last full backup and the most recent differential backup are required. This reduces the dependency on a long chain of backup files and lowers the risk of recovery failure due to a missing or damaged backup segment.

Both incremental and differential backups play important roles in achieving an organization's recovery time objectives and recovery point objectives. Recovery time objective, or RTO, defines the maximum acceptable time to restore service after a failure, while recovery point objective, or RPO, indicates the maximum tolerable amount of data loss measured in time. Incremental backups support more aggressive RPOs because they can be scheduled frequently throughout the day, sometimes as often as every few minutes, without putting excessive strain on the system. Differential backups, while larger and less frequent, offer faster RTOs because fewer files are needed for a complete restore. The optimal approach often involves a hybrid strategy that combines daily full backups, hourly differential backups during peak hours, and incremental backups during off-peak periods.

Database engines implement these backup methods in various ways, often providing built-in tools and configurations to automate the process. Some systems use block-level tracking, identifying changed data blocks to minimize backup size. Others use transaction log-based methods, capturing logical changes such as inserts, updates, and deletes. In block-level systems, restoring involves reconstructing the original file by merging the blocks from the base backup with the blocks from the incremental or differential layers. In log-based systems, recovery is performed by replaying the transactions recorded in the backup files. Each approach has implications for performance, storage requirements, and the precision of point-in-time recovery.

Scheduling and retention policies are essential in managing incremental and differential backups. Retention defines how long each backup is kept before being deleted or archived. A typical policy might retain daily incrementals for seven days, weekly differentials for one month, and monthly full backups for a year. These policies must be aligned with compliance regulations, business continuity requirements, and storage capacity. Long chains of incremental backups may require more frequent verification to ensure that each link remains intact and usable. In environments where changes occur rapidly, long-term differential backups may grow excessively large, reducing their effectiveness and requiring adjustments to the backup schedule.

Monitoring and verification are vital to the success of any incremental or differential backup strategy. Backups should not only be completed successfully but also be verified for integrity and tested regularly through simulated restores. Automated tools can check for checksum mismatches, file corruption, and missing links in the backup chain. Alerting mechanisms should notify administrators of any anomalies, such as failed backup jobs, unusually large backup sizes, or delays in scheduled tasks. Regular testing ensures that backup procedures are reliable and that recovery can be performed under pressure when the need arises.

Storage and network considerations also influence the choice between incremental and differential backups. Incremental backups minimize storage use and reduce the load on storage systems, making them ideal for environments with limited capacity or expensive storage tiers. They also consume less network bandwidth when transferred offsite, which is especially important in distributed environments or cloud-based infrastructures. Differential backups, while larger, can still offer storage advantages over repeated full backups and are easier to manage in situations where restore speed is critical. Compression and deduplication technologies can further reduce the size of both types of backups, though they may introduce additional processing overhead.

Encryption and security are important for protecting backup data, especially in environments with sensitive or regulated information. Both incremental and differential backups should be encrypted in transit and at rest using strong, industry-standard encryption algorithms. Access to backup files must be controlled through role-based access policies, and audit trails should be maintained to track who accessed the data and when. Encrypted backups must be paired with reliable key management practices to ensure that data can be decrypted during restoration and that keys are not lost or compromised.

Disaster recovery planning relies heavily on the use of incremental and differential backups. In the event of a catastrophic failure, such as a hardware crash, ransomware attack, or data center outage, the ability to quickly restore the system to a recent and consistent state can make the difference between a minor disruption and a prolonged outage. By integrating these backup types into a structured recovery plan, organizations gain flexibility, reduce downtime, and ensure that data is protected across multiple time horizons. When used effectively, incremental and differential backups are more than just technical conveniences—they are fundamental safeguards for business continuity and resilience.

Automating Backup Processes

Automating backup processes is a critical step in ensuring data protection, consistency, and reliability in modern database systems. Manual backup procedures, while feasible in small environments, are error-prone, time-consuming, and not scalable. As systems grow in complexity and data volumes increase, automation becomes essential to guarantee that backups occur regularly, efficiently, and without human oversight. A properly automated backup solution not only performs scheduled data copies but also integrates monitoring, validation, alerting, and reporting mechanisms. These elements work together to create a resilient and repeatable system that supports disaster recovery, data integrity, and compliance requirements with minimal administrative effort.

At the heart of automation lies the scheduling mechanism. This involves setting up recurring jobs that initiate full, incremental, or differential backups according to a predefined timetable. Tools for scheduling backups vary by platform and can include native database schedulers, operating system cron jobs, task schedulers, or enterprise backup software with graphical user interfaces. The scheduling should align with the organization's recovery objectives, data change frequency, and workload patterns. For example, full backups may run weekly during off-peak hours, while incremental backups execute multiple times per day to capture rapid changes without overloading the system. Ensuring that backups do not conflict with high-usage periods requires careful planning and analysis of system load profiles.

Automating the execution of backup jobs involves scripting or configuring commands that initiate backup operations. These commands typically specify parameters such as the type of backup, the location where the backup files should be stored, and the format or compression settings to use. Modern databases often support command-line tools or APIs that enable such automation. Scripts can be written in shell, PowerShell, or programming languages such as Python to provide logic, error handling, and integration with other system components. These scripts should include steps to verify that the database is in a consistent state before backing up and to capture relevant metadata, such as timestamps, file sizes, and checksums, which are useful for validation.

Error handling is a crucial aspect of automation. Backup scripts must be able to detect failures and respond appropriately, whether by retrying the operation, logging the error, or triggering an alert. Common reasons for backup failures include lack of disk space, permission issues, network timeouts, and database locks. By anticipating these conditions and coding responses into the automation logic, administrators can reduce the risk of silent failures that go unnoticed until a restore is needed. Proper use of exit codes, logging frameworks, and exception handling constructs ensures that failures are visible and actionable.

Monitoring and alerting systems complement automation by providing real-time feedback on backup status. Integrating backup processes with centralized monitoring tools allows administrators to track job execution, success rates, duration, and system resource usage. Dashboards can display trends over time, helping to identify slowdowns or anomalies. Alerts should be sent via email, SMS, or messaging platforms when backup jobs fail, run longer than expected, or produce incomplete files. Advanced monitoring can also verify that backups meet compliance requirements, such as encryption, retention, and geographic distribution.

Automated validation of backup files adds an additional layer of protection. This step involves verifying that the backup files are complete, uncorrupted, and restorable. Validation can be performed by checking checksums, comparing file sizes, or executing test restores in a sandbox environment. Some enterprise backup tools include built-in verification features that automatically simulate restores to verify data integrity. Incorporating validation into the backup process ensures that corrupted or incomplete backups are detected early, reducing the risk of data loss during an actual recovery event.

Retention and cleanup policies should also be automated. Backup files consume storage space, and without proper management, they can quickly fill disks, slow down backup jobs, and increase costs. Automating the removal of expired backups according to retention policies helps maintain a balance between data availability and storage efficiency. Retention policies may vary by backup type, with full backups kept for longer periods than incremental or differential ones. Some organizations implement tiered storage strategies where recent backups are stored on fast, local storage, while older backups are moved to slower, archival systems such as tape libraries or cloud cold storage.

Integration with version control and change management systems enhances the reliability of backup automation. Backup scripts, configuration files, and documentation should be maintained in a version-controlled repository, enabling teams to track changes, audit modifications, and roll back to known-good configurations. Change management processes ensure that updates to the backup system are tested, reviewed, and deployed in a controlled manner, reducing the likelihood of introducing errors or regressions. Automation tools can be tied into deployment pipelines, automatically updating backup configurations when new databases or servers are added to the environment.

Security must be a top priority in automated backup systems. Backup scripts and tools often require elevated privileges to access sensitive data, and these credentials must be protected through secure vaults or encryption. Backup files themselves should be encrypted both in transit and at rest, especially when stored offsite or in the cloud. Automation tools should ensure that backups are only accessible to authorized personnel and that all actions are logged for auditing purposes. Automated processes should also include checks to verify that encryption is applied correctly and that access permissions are enforced consistently.

Cloud-native environments introduce new challenges and opportunities for backup automation. Many cloud providers offer managed database services with built-in backup features that can be configured and scheduled through APIs or management consoles. Automation in these environments may involve provisioning backups across multiple regions, integrating with identity and access management systems, and ensuring compliance with data sovereignty regulations. Hybrid environments, where on-premises systems coexist with cloud databases, require orchestration tools capable of managing diverse platforms and consolidating backup data into a unified recovery strategy.

Ultimately, the goal of automating backup processes is to reduce risk, save time, and provide consistent, reliable protection for organizational data. By eliminating manual steps, enforcing best practices, and integrating with monitoring and validation systems, automation transforms backup from a reactive task into a proactive component of operational resilience. As data volumes grow and system complexity increases, automation ensures that backups keep pace with demands and remain a dependable safeguard against loss, corruption, or disaster. The confidence gained from knowing that backups are performed accurately, on schedule, and with verifiable results is invaluable in any modern data-driven enterprise.

Testing and Verifying Backups

Testing and verifying backups is one of the most crucial but often overlooked aspects of a reliable data protection strategy. While creating backups is a foundational part of safeguarding data, merely having backup files is not enough to ensure recoverability. Backups can fail silently, become corrupted, be incomplete, or be stored in an unusable format. If these problems are not detected before a disaster occurs, an organization could face catastrophic data loss despite having what it believed to be a robust backup system. Therefore, regular and rigorous testing and verification of backups is not a luxury but a necessity. It transforms backup from a passive safety net into an active, dependable component of business continuity.

The primary goal of testing backups is to confirm that data can actually be restored from them, accurately and within the expected recovery time. Verification should be conducted on multiple levels. The first level involves checking the completion status of backup jobs. Backup systems typically generate logs indicating whether a job succeeded or failed, along with performance metrics such as backup duration and data volume. However, a successful job status does not guarantee a usable backup. It only confirms that the process ran to completion according to its configuration. If that configuration was incorrect or the underlying storage had issues, the resulting backup may be unusable despite the success report.

A deeper level of verification includes validating the integrity of the backup files themselves. This process checks whether the files are complete, uncorrupted, and match the expected structure. Techniques such as checksums, hash comparisons, and file size verification can identify subtle problems like silent data corruption, incomplete writes, or storage anomalies. Some backup systems offer built-in integrity checks that automatically validate the data during or immediately after the backup process. These tools provide an essential first line of defense but should be supplemented by independent validation methods, especially when compliance, legal obligations, or high-value data are involved.

The most effective and thorough verification method is performing actual restore tests. This involves restoring data from backup files into a test environment and verifying that the restored data is complete, consistent, and functional. The test environment should mimic the production environment as closely as possible, including the same operating system, database software, and configurations. Restoration tests can be performed at various levels of granularity, from restoring an entire system or database to recovering individual tables, files, or transaction logs. Each of these tests verifies not only the data itself but also the procedures, scripts, and personnel involved in the recovery process.

Restore testing also reveals bottlenecks, configuration issues, and hidden dependencies that might affect the speed and reliability of an actual recovery. For example, a restore might fail because of missing credentials, incompatible software versions, insufficient disk space, or network latency. Identifying and resolving these problems during a planned test is far less costly and disruptive than encountering them during a real incident. Restore testing also validates the organization's recovery time objective and recovery point objective by measuring how long it takes to recover and how much data is lost in the process. These insights allow organizations to refine their backup frequency, storage strategies, and resource allocation to better align with business needs.

Testing should not be a one-time or occasional event but a regular part of operational procedures. The frequency of testing depends on the criticality of the data and the rate at which it changes. Highly dynamic systems may require daily or weekly validation, while less volatile systems can be tested monthly or quarterly. Automation tools can help schedule and execute restore tests without requiring constant manual intervention. These tools can restore test snapshots, run automated checks on the restored data, and alert administrators to discrepancies. Automated testing makes it feasible to maintain a continuous level of assurance across a large number of systems and backup sets.

Versioning and labeling of backups are essential to support testing and tracking. Each backup should be clearly marked with metadata indicating when it was created, what it contains, and which system or environment it corresponds to. This information is critical during both testing and actual recovery scenarios to ensure that the correct backup is selected. In complex environments with many interconnected systems, dependencies between backup sets must be documented and understood. Testing helps validate that restoring one component, such as a database, does not fail because of missing elements in another, such as the application server or configuration files.

Documentation plays a vital role in backup testing. Every test should be documented in detail, including the backup source, the restore process, any issues encountered, and the final outcome. These records create a valuable knowledge base that supports training, audits, and continuous improvement. They also provide a reference during high-pressure recovery situations, when accurate information and clear procedures can prevent costly mistakes. Backup testing procedures should be included in disaster recovery plans, reviewed during security assessments, and updated whenever changes are made to systems, applications, or data structures.

Security considerations must be addressed during testing as well. Restoring production data into a test environment can expose sensitive information if the test environment is not properly secured. Access to restored data must be tightly controlled, and anonymization or masking techniques should be used when appropriate. Logging and auditing should capture all access to test data, and test environments should be isolated from the production network to prevent accidental interference or data leakage. Security policies should clearly define who is authorized to perform testing and what controls must be in place before testing begins.

Testing and verifying backups ensures that an organization's investments in data protection are not wasted. It builds confidence that recovery will work when it is needed most and reveals vulnerabilities that can be corrected before they become liabilities. In an age where data is among the most valuable assets an organization holds, the ability to protect, recover, and trust that data is fundamental to operational resilience. Without regular testing, even the most advanced backup system is built on uncertain ground. By making testing a disciplined and automated part of the backup lifecycle, organizations move from hope to certainty in their disaster recovery capabilities.

Disaster Recovery Planning

Disaster recovery planning is a critical discipline within database management that ensures the continuity and restoration of operations after catastrophic events. These events can range from hardware failures and software bugs to cyberattacks, natural disasters, and human error. Without a solid disaster recovery plan in place, organizations risk extended downtime, loss of critical data, financial loss, and reputational damage. A well-designed disaster recovery strategy defines not only how to recover from specific incidents but also how to prepare systems, data, processes, and personnel to act quickly and effectively when disaster strikes. It transforms a reactive process into a proactive, structured response that minimizes impact and supports business resilience.

At the core of any disaster recovery plan is a clear understanding of what needs to be protected and what the acceptable levels of risk are. This begins with identifying critical assets, including databases, application servers, storage systems, and network infrastructure. Each asset is evaluated based on its importance to business operations, the data it holds, and the potential consequences of its unavailability. From this analysis, two essential metrics are established: the recovery time objective and the recovery point objective. The recovery time objective defines how quickly systems and services must be restored to maintain business continuity. The recovery point objective determines the maximum amount of data loss that can be tolerated, measured in time.

These objectives shape the design of backup strategies, failover mechanisms, and infrastructure investments.

A comprehensive disaster recovery plan must include detailed documentation of all backup processes and systems. This includes the locations of backup files, the frequency and type of backups performed, the tools and scripts used, and the retention policies in place. It must specify how backups are verified, tested, and secured. Knowing that backup data exists is not enough; the plan must ensure that the data is accurate, current, and accessible under emergency conditions. Regular restore tests should be scheduled and documented to validate that data can be recovered within the required timeframes. The plan must also include procedures for handling scenarios where primary data centers become inaccessible, requiring restoration from offsite or cloud-based storage.

Replication and high availability technologies play an important role in disaster recovery planning. For mission-critical systems, active-passive or active-active replication between geographically separated data centers can reduce downtime to near zero. These systems continuously replicate data in real time or near-real time, allowing operations to switch to a backup site if the primary location fails. Implementing replication requires careful configuration to avoid data divergence, network bottlenecks, or replication lag. For less critical systems, asynchronous replication or scheduled data exports may be sufficient, with the understanding that some data loss may occur in the event of a failure. The plan must clearly define which systems are protected by which methods, and what recovery guarantees are associated with each.

The human element is another vital component of disaster recovery planning. Even the most advanced technical solutions can fail if people do not know how to use them. The plan must identify key personnel responsible for executing recovery tasks, along with their contact information and roles during an incident. It should include step-by-step instructions for declaring a disaster, initiating failover procedures, restoring backups, verifying data integrity, and returning systems to normal operations. These instructions must be kept up to date and reviewed regularly to reflect changes in infrastructure, personnel, and business processes. Training and drills should be conducted periodically to ensure that staff are familiar with their responsibilities and can perform them under pressure.

Communication is equally important during a disaster. The plan must define how internal and external stakeholders will be informed, what messages will be conveyed, and who is authorized to speak on behalf of the organization. Clear communication reduces confusion, maintains customer confidence, and ensures that regulatory bodies and partners are kept informed. The plan should include templates for emergency messages, press releases, and status updates. Communication channels must be resilient, with backups for email, phone systems, and internet connectivity. If standard tools are unavailable, alternatives such as satellite phones or secure messaging apps should be outlined in the plan.

Security considerations must be embedded into disaster recovery planning. Disasters often create vulnerabilities that attackers can exploit. Recovery procedures must include steps to verify the integrity of systems and data, to apply patches if needed, and to monitor for suspicious activity during and after restoration. The plan should define how to handle incidents caused by cyber threats, including ransomware attacks and data breaches. In such scenarios, recovery may involve isolating affected systems, analyzing malware, restoring from clean backups, and conducting forensic investigations. Ensuring that recovery systems themselves are not compromised is essential, requiring secure storage, access controls, and encryption.

Regulatory compliance is another dimension of disaster recovery planning. Many industries are subject to legal and contractual obligations regarding data retention, recovery time, and breach notification. The plan must account for these requirements, documenting how compliance is maintained even during a disaster. This may involve demonstrating that backups are retained for a specified period, that they are stored in approved geographic locations, and that recovery times meet regulatory expectations. Auditors may require evidence of testing, training, and procedural documentation. Keeping detailed records of all disaster recovery activities, including drills and actual incidents, helps fulfill these obligations and supports accountability.

The effectiveness of a disaster recovery plan is measured not only by how quickly systems are restored but by how smoothly the entire process unfolds. After each drill or real incident, a post-mortem review should be conducted to assess what worked well, what went wrong, and how the plan can be improved. These reviews are opportunities to refine procedures, update documentation, and enhance infrastructure. They should involve all stakeholders, including technical staff, business leaders, and compliance officers. Continuous improvement ensures that the disaster recovery plan evolves alongside the organization and remains relevant in the face of new threats and technologies.

Disaster recovery planning is not a one-time project but a continuous process of assessment, preparation, and refinement. It requires input from across the organization and must be championed by leadership to receive the necessary attention and resources. As digital systems become more complex and interconnected, the risk of disruption grows. Having a tested, well-documented, and clearly communicated disaster recovery plan is no longer optional but essential. It provides the structure and confidence needed to respond swiftly to unexpected events, minimize damage, and restore operations with minimal interruption. In a world where downtime is measured in lost revenue, missed opportunities, and damaged trust, disaster recovery planning becomes a vital pillar of organizational resilience.

High Availability Architecture

High availability architecture is a foundational principle in modern database systems, designed to ensure continuous operation and minimal downtime even in the face of hardware failures, software bugs, network outages, or maintenance tasks. As organizations become increasingly reliant on data-driven applications and real-time services, any disruption to database availability can lead to loss of revenue, damaged reputation, and failure to meet service level agreements. High availability goes beyond basic redundancy by enabling systems to detect failures quickly, recover gracefully, and resume operations with minimal human intervention. It is a comprehensive approach that encompasses hardware, software, networking, and process design to create a resilient infrastructure capable of withstanding failures and maintaining service continuity.

At the core of high availability architecture is redundancy. Every critical component of the database system must have a failover counterpart ready to take over if the primary fails. This includes database instances, storage systems, network links, and even data centers. Redundancy can be implemented in different configurations depending on the specific requirements of performance, cost, and recovery time. Active-passive configurations are common, where one node actively handles the workload while a secondary node remains on standby, continuously receiving updates. When a failure is detected, the passive node is promoted to active, ensuring that service is restored quickly. Active-active configurations go further by allowing multiple nodes to process requests simultaneously, distributing the load and offering higher throughput along with high availability. This approach requires careful synchronization and conflict resolution but offers the added benefit of performance scaling.

Automatic failover mechanisms are essential in high availability systems. These mechanisms monitor the health of primary components and initiate switchover procedures when problems are detected. Health checks are typically performed through heartbeat signals or periodic probes that test connectivity, response time, and system metrics. If a component fails to respond within a defined threshold, the failover process begins, which may involve promoting a standby server, re-routing traffic through updated DNS records or load balancers, and restoring in-memory data or cached sessions. This process must be fast and reliable to ensure that users experience minimal disruption. Orchestration tools and clustering software often handle the failover logic, managing the complexity of synchronization, consistency, and resource allocation across nodes.

Data replication is another critical element of high availability architecture. To enable failover without data loss, replicas of the database must be kept up to date with changes from the primary system. This replication can be synchronous or asynchronous. In synchronous replication, changes are written to both the primary and the replica before the transaction is considered committed. This guarantees zero data loss at the cost of increased latency.

Asynchronous replication, on the other hand, allows the primary to commit changes immediately while the replica catches up, reducing latency but introducing a risk of data loss during failover. The choice between these approaches depends on the balance between performance requirements and tolerance for potential data loss.

Geographic distribution further enhances high availability by protecting against site-level failures. In this model, multiple data centers in different geographic regions host redundant systems, allowing service continuity even in the event of natural disasters, power outages, or regional network failures. Geo-redundancy introduces additional challenges such as data consistency, latency, and compliance with data residency laws. Techniques such as distributed consensus algorithms, eventual consistency models, and conflict resolution policies are employed to manage these complexities. Multi-region architectures often incorporate intelligent routing based on user location, latency, or availability to ensure optimal performance and resilience.

Storage systems in high availability architectures must also be designed for fault tolerance. Shared storage solutions like network-attached storage or storage area networks offer centralized data access with redundancy features such as RAID configurations, replication, and snapshotting. Alternatively, modern architectures increasingly favor distributed storage systems that replicate data across nodes and offer high durability and availability without a single point of failure. These systems use techniques like erasure coding, quorum writes, and self-healing mechanisms to maintain integrity and performance even when individual components fail.

Networking plays a crucial role in high availability. Load balancers distribute incoming traffic across multiple database nodes, ensuring that no single node becomes overwhelmed and that failed nodes are automatically bypassed. Redundant network paths, switches, and routers prevent single points of failure in the communication layer. DNS failover services can quickly redirect traffic to healthy endpoints when issues are detected. Security appliances such as firewalls and intrusion detection systems must also be included in the high availability design, with redundant configurations and synchronization to prevent them from becoming bottlenecks or vulnerabilities during failover events.

Monitoring and alerting are essential for maintaining high availability. Continuous visibility into system health, performance, and error rates allows administrators to detect and resolve issues before they escalate into outages. Monitoring systems should track metrics such as replication lag, disk I/O, memory usage, query performance, and network latency. Alerts must be actionable and routed to on-call personnel or automation systems capable of taking corrective action. Predictive analytics can identify trends that indicate impending failures, enabling preemptive maintenance or resource scaling to avoid downtime.

Maintenance procedures must be carefully designed in high availability environments. Routine tasks such as patching, upgrades, and configuration changes must be performed in a rolling manner that avoids taking the entire system offline. Blue-green deployments, canary releases, and live migrations allow administrators to apply changes incrementally and verify stability before proceeding. Backup systems must be compatible with high availability configurations, ensuring that snapshots and backups do not interfere with replication or performance. Testing failover procedures regularly in controlled conditions validates the readiness of the system and the staff to handle real-world incidents.

High availability is not achieved through technology alone but through disciplined planning, documentation, and training. Every aspect of the architecture must be thoroughly documented, including topology diagrams, failover procedures, and recovery plans. Runbooks must be created and maintained to guide teams through incident response. All team members should be trained to understand the architecture, their roles during failover events, and the tools available to them. High availability is a shared responsibility across development, operations, and security teams, requiring collaboration and a culture of resilience.

The investment in high availability architecture yields substantial benefits. It provides assurance that critical applications and services will remain operational under adverse conditions, reduces the financial and reputational impact of downtime, and supports compliance with service level agreements and regulatory requirements. As systems become more complex and user expectations for uptime grow, high availability is no longer a luxury reserved for mission-critical systems but a baseline requirement for any service that demands trust and reliability. A well-designed high availability architecture combines technical excellence, proactive monitoring, and coordinated human response to deliver continuous service in a world where disruption is always a possibility.

Using Cloud Services for Backup and Restore

The use of cloud services for backup and restore has transformed traditional data protection strategies by offering scalable, cost-effective, and resilient solutions that overcome the limitations of on-premises infrastructure. Cloud platforms provide a flexible environment where data can be stored securely, accessed from multiple locations, and recovered efficiently in case of loss or failure. As organizations increasingly move toward hybrid and fully cloud-native architectures, integrating cloud-based backup and restore mechanisms becomes essential for achieving operational continuity and regulatory compliance. The key advantage of using cloud services lies in their ability to abstract complex infrastructure while delivering high durability, geographic redundancy, and automated management features that support modern business needs.

At the foundation of cloud-based backup systems is the concept of storage-as-a-service, where providers such as Amazon Web Services, Microsoft Azure, and Google Cloud Platform offer durable object storage solutions like Amazon S3, Azure Blob Storage, or Google Cloud Storage. These services are designed to store large volumes of data with redundancy across multiple physical devices and often across geographically dispersed locations. By leveraging such platforms, organizations can ensure that backup data is not only safe from hardware failures but also resilient against regional disasters. This inherent redundancy provides a level of durability that is difficult and expensive to achieve with traditional on-premises hardware.

One of the primary motivations for adopting cloud services for backup is scalability. Traditional backup systems often face challenges in managing growing data volumes, requiring frequent hardware upgrades, expanded storage arrays, or increased administrative effort. Cloud platforms eliminate these concerns by providing virtually unlimited storage capacity that grows automatically as data is added. Organizations no longer need to predict future capacity needs or invest in excess infrastructure. Instead, they can take advantage of pay-as-you-go pricing models that align costs with actual usage, making backup more affordable and predictable.

Cloud services also simplify the process of automating backup operations. Providers offer tools and APIs that enable scheduled backups, lifecycle policies, and data tiering. For example, administrators can configure backups to run daily and automatically transition older data to lower-cost storage tiers such as Amazon S3 Glacier or Azure Archive Storage. These archival options offer significant savings for long-term retention while preserving access when needed. Backup policies can be enforced across multiple systems and environments, ensuring consistent protection regardless of whether workloads reside on-premises, in virtual machines, or in containerized cloud-native services.

Security is a critical component of cloud-based backup and restore strategies. Leading cloud providers incorporate advanced security measures, including encryption at rest and in transit, identity and access management, audit logging, and compliance certifications. Encryption ensures that data is protected from unauthorized access, while fine-grained access controls allow organizations to define who can view or modify backup data. Multi-factor authentication and key management systems enhance protection by reducing the risk of credential compromise. Cloud services also support immutable storage, which prevents backups from being deleted or modified for a specified retention period. This feature is particularly valuable in defending against ransomware attacks, where local backup files are often targeted and encrypted along with primary data.

The flexibility of cloud platforms extends to restore operations as well. Cloud services allow for selective or full data recovery, supporting use cases such as granular object restoration, system-level disaster recovery, and migration between environments. With infrastructure-as-code and automated deployment tools, administrators can rapidly spin up new instances in the cloud and restore data from backups without manual intervention. This accelerates recovery time objectives and minimizes downtime. For hybrid deployments, cloud services enable restoration to either cloud-based systems or on-premises environments, offering agility in how and where data is recovered.

Cloud-native databases, such as Amazon RDS, Google Cloud SQL, and Azure SQL Database, offer integrated backup and restore capabilities managed entirely by the provider. These services handle backup scheduling, encryption, replication, and retention automatically, reducing the burden on database administrators. Point-in-time recovery is often included, allowing users to restore a database to any second within a configured window, typically up to thirty-five days. This functionality is essential for recovering from user errors, data corruption, or unintended changes. The ease with which these backups can be initiated, monitored, and restored enhances reliability and allows teams to focus on higher-value tasks.

Using cloud services for backup also supports regulatory and governance needs. Many industries require data to be retained for specific periods and stored in particular geographic regions. Cloud providers offer controls for setting data residency, managing retention schedules, and generating audit reports. Data classification and tagging further enhance compliance by enabling organizations to identify sensitive information and apply appropriate protection levels. Integration with governance tools helps enforce policies consistently across multiple cloud accounts, projects, or tenants, supporting a unified approach to data protection.

Monitoring and observability are essential in cloud backup systems. Dashboards and reporting tools provided by cloud platforms allow administrators to track backup status, storage consumption, job success rates, and anomalies. Alerts can be configured to notify teams when backups fail, exceed expected duration, or result in incomplete files. These monitoring capabilities ensure that issues are detected and addressed promptly before they escalate into serious incidents. In addition, many cloud services offer integrations with centralized logging and analytics platforms, enabling organizations to correlate backup data with operational metrics and incident response systems.

Despite the many benefits, adopting cloud services for backup and restore requires careful planning. Organizations must assess bandwidth limitations, especially when transferring large volumes of data to and from the cloud. Network optimization techniques such as compression, deduplication, and scheduled transfers during off-peak hours help mitigate these challenges. It is also important to consider vendor lock-in and ensure that backup data can be exported or migrated to other platforms if needed. Adopting open formats and using tools that support multiple cloud providers can increase portability and reduce long-term risk.

Ultimately, cloud-based backup and restore solutions provide organizations with a powerful toolkit for protecting data in an increasingly complex digital landscape. By leveraging the scalability, security, automation, and resilience offered by cloud services, businesses can create robust backup strategies that meet operational, regulatory, and budgetary requirements. Whether used as a primary backup solution or as part of a hybrid strategy that includes on-premises infrastructure, cloud services enable faster recovery, better visibility, and improved agility in responding to data loss events. As threats to data continue to evolve, the ability to store, protect, and recover critical information in the cloud becomes a strategic advantage that no modern organization can afford to overlook.

Performance Tuning Methodologies

Performance tuning methodologies in database systems are essential for maintaining efficient query execution, reducing resource consumption, and ensuring scalability as data volumes and user activity grow. These methodologies encompass a broad set of practices, analytical approaches, and corrective techniques aimed at identifying bottlenecks and optimizing various components of a database environment. Tuning performance is not a one-time activity but a continuous process that adapts to changing workloads, system configurations, and business requirements. The overarching goal is to achieve consistent, predictable, and fast responses to queries while minimizing the impact on system resources such as CPU, memory, disk I/O, and network throughput.

The first step in any performance tuning process is proper identification of performance issues. This requires systematic observation, measurement, and analysis of system behavior. Relying on assumptions or superficial metrics often leads to misguided efforts and ineffective changes. Database administrators begin by collecting baseline performance data, which includes query response times, execution plans, I/O statistics, CPU usage, memory allocation, and wait events. These metrics provide insight into where time is being spent during query execution and which resources are under pressure. Tools such as query profilers, system monitors, and execution plan analyzers are indispensable in this phase, offering visibility into internal operations and helping pinpoint the root causes of slowdowns.

Once an issue has been identified, the next phase involves isolating the scope of the problem. Performance issues can originate from poorly written queries, suboptimal indexing, inefficient execution plans, locking and contention, hardware limitations, or configuration missteps. A methodical approach to isolation helps distinguish between symptoms and causes. For example, a high CPU usage metric might indicate an inefficient query plan with full table scans or nested loop joins on large datasets. However, the underlying cause could be missing indexes, outdated statistics, or inappropriate join conditions. Correct diagnosis enables targeted fixes and avoids unnecessary changes that might introduce new problems.

Query optimization is a central focus of performance tuning. SQL queries must be carefully crafted to take advantage of available indexes, minimize unnecessary data access, and avoid expensive operations such as full scans or excessive joins. The optimizer plays a crucial role in determining the most efficient execution strategy based on available statistics, schema design, and query structure. Reviewing and understanding the execution plan is essential for evaluating how the optimizer interprets the query and which operations contribute most to cost and latency. Adjustments to query syntax, hints, join order, or filters can significantly alter execution plans and improve performance. Tuning often involves rewriting queries to be more selective, reducing the number of rows processed, or replacing correlated subqueries with joins.

Indexing strategies are another major component of performance tuning. Indexes provide fast access paths to data, but they must be used judiciously to balance read performance against write overhead. Creating indexes on frequently filtered or joined columns can drastically reduce I/O and CPU consumption. However, excessive or redundant indexes increase storage requirements and slow down insert, update, and delete operations. Periodic index analysis helps identify unused or fragmented indexes, and automated tools can recommend index additions or removals based on query patterns. Covering indexes that include all columns needed by a query can eliminate lookups and further speed up execution. Partitioned indexes and filtered indexes also offer advanced control in high-volume systems.

Memory and buffer pool tuning are essential for optimizing how data is read, cached, and reused. Properly sized memory allocation reduces the need for disk access and accelerates query execution. Buffer pools should be large enough to hold frequently accessed pages, and configuration parameters must be adjusted based on workload characteristics. In systems with high concurrency, additional tuning may be required to prevent memory pressure and contention for shared resources. Monitoring cache hit ratios, page reads, and evictions provides insight into memory efficiency. Adjustments to memory management strategies can reduce latency and improve throughput for both transactional and analytical workloads.

Concurrency control and transaction isolation levels also affect performance. While high isolation levels ensure consistency, they can lead to locking, blocking, and deadlocks in busy systems. Tuning involves selecting the appropriate isolation level for each use case and designing transactions to be short, efficient, and non-conflicting. Techniques such as row versioning, snapshot isolation, and optimistic concurrency can improve performance by reducing contention. Deadlock detection and resolution mechanisms should be monitored and optimized to ensure that conflicts are resolved quickly without impacting user experience.

Storage configuration is another area of tuning that is often overlooked. The layout of database files on disk, choice of file systems, RAID configurations, and IOPS capacity all influence performance. Distributing data across multiple disks or storage arrays reduces contention and increases parallelism. In cloud environments, selecting the appropriate storage tier, provisioning throughput, and using caching layers can significantly affect performance. Monitoring disk queues, latency, and throughput helps identify bottlenecks and informs decisions about storage upgrades or reconfiguration.

Database configuration settings play a critical role in tuning. Parameters such as connection pool sizes, parallelism settings, query timeouts, and logging levels must be tuned to match the workload. Defaults provided by the database engine may not be suitable for every environment, especially as systems scale. Fine-tuning these settings requires a deep understanding of how the database engine allocates resources and schedules operations. Performance testing in a controlled environment helps validate changes before applying them to production.

Workload management and query prioritization are advanced techniques for environments with mixed workloads. Resource governor features in some database systems allow administrators to define rules for allocating CPU, memory, and I/O bandwidth based on user roles, application types, or query complexity. This ensures that high-priority tasks receive sufficient resources while preventing background jobs or poorly written queries from degrading system performance. Monitoring tools must be integrated into this strategy to detect anomalies and enforce resource policies dynamically.

Performance tuning methodologies also benefit from automation and machine learning. Some modern database engines include self-tuning capabilities that monitor system behavior, learn from query patterns, and make recommendations or adjustments in real time. These features reduce the manual burden on administrators and adapt quickly to changing workloads. However, automated tuning should be supplemented with human oversight to validate changes and maintain control over critical systems.

Effective performance tuning is iterative and data-driven. It requires continuous monitoring, proactive analysis, and a structured methodology for identifying, isolating, and resolving performance issues. Collaboration between developers, DBAs, and infrastructure teams is essential to understand the broader context of performance challenges and to implement solutions that are sustainable, scalable, and aligned with business objectives. By embracing systematic tuning practices, organizations can ensure that their database systems remain responsive, efficient, and capable of supporting growing demands with confidence and control.

Monitoring Tools and Metrics

Monitoring tools and metrics are essential components of effective database management, providing the visibility and insight necessary to maintain performance, detect anomalies, and ensure availability across complex environments. As data systems scale and workloads become increasingly dynamic, the ability to observe internal operations in real time and retrospectively becomes a critical advantage. Monitoring is not merely about collecting statistics but about transforming those statistics into actionable intelligence. With accurate monitoring in place, database administrators can anticipate problems before they occur, respond quickly when issues arise, and make informed decisions to optimize and secure the system over time.

The foundation of any monitoring strategy begins with identifying the key metrics that define the health and performance of a database. These metrics are gathered across several domains, including system resources, query performance, storage behavior, network activity, and user interactions. CPU utilization, memory consumption, and disk I/O are core system-level indicators that help determine how efficiently hardware resources are being used. High CPU usage may signal expensive queries or contention in the query processor, while memory usage patterns reveal the effectiveness of caching and buffer pool configurations. Disk I/O statistics are particularly important, as databases are fundamentally I/O-intensive applications. Excessive read or write latency may indicate inadequate storage performance or poorly optimized access patterns.

Query metrics offer a detailed view into the workload profile and are central to diagnosing performance issues. These include query execution time, number of rows scanned or returned, execution plan statistics, and wait events. Monitoring long-running queries, high-frequency queries, and queries with high resource usage helps identify candidates for optimization. Tools that capture and analyze execution plans are invaluable, as they allow administrators to understand how the database engine interprets and processes SQL statements. Observing changes in query plans over time can also highlight the effects of schema changes, index modifications, or statistics updates, enabling proactive tuning before performance degrades.

Concurrency and locking metrics provide insight into how multiple users and applications interact with the database. Metrics such as transaction throughput, deadlock frequency, lock wait times, and active session counts help assess the system's ability to handle concurrent operations. High lock contention or frequent deadlocks often point to issues in application design, inappropriate isolation levels, or poorly tuned transactions. Monitoring these metrics over time allows teams to refine transaction strategies, apply optimistic or pessimistic locking mechanisms where appropriate, and ensure that the database can scale with user demand.

Storage monitoring is another critical aspect of database observability. Metrics such as table and index size, fragmentation levels, free space availability, and growth trends help ensure that the database does not run out of capacity unexpectedly. Tracking write-ahead logs, transaction logs, and temporary storage usage is also essential for understanding the internal activity of the database engine. Log file saturation, excessive checkpoint activity, or abnormal growth of temporary files may indicate inefficient queries or excessive write operations that require investigation. In cloud environments, monitoring storage consumption directly impacts costs, so visibility into data growth and tiered storage usage supports budget control.

Replication and high availability configurations introduce additional metrics that must be observed. In replicated environments, metrics such as replication lag, transaction latency, and synchronization status are critical for ensuring data consistency and timely failover. High replication lag can result in stale data on read replicas, potentially affecting application behavior and user experience. Monitoring the state of primary and standby nodes, replication health, and failover readiness is vital for disaster recovery planning and operational continuity. These metrics must be paired with alerting mechanisms that notify administrators when thresholds are breached or when the system drifts from its desired state.

Modern monitoring tools offer real-time dashboards, historical trend analysis, and advanced alerting capabilities. These tools can be platform-specific, such as Oracle Enterprise Manager, SQL Server Management Studio, or PostgreSQL's pg_stat family of views, or platform-agnostic solutions like Prometheus, Grafana, Datadog, or New Relic. These tools often integrate with the operating system, cloud provider, and application stack, offering a holistic view of the database in context. A good monitoring tool not only visualizes metrics but enables threshold-based alerts, anomaly detection, and intelligent recommendations based on historical patterns and learned behaviors.

Effective monitoring extends to the network layer, especially in distributed systems or cloud-based deployments. Metrics such as connection counts, network latency, packet loss, and throughput are important for diagnosing connectivity issues that affect database availability and query response times. Monitoring the number of active connections, connection pool usage, and failed login attempts also supports security and access control objectives. Identifying unexpected spikes in connection activity may signal application misbehavior, denial-of-service attacks, or misconfigured load balancers.

Security monitoring is an increasingly important aspect of database observability. Tracking access logs, audit trails, privilege changes, and failed authentication attempts helps detect unauthorized access and potential security breaches. Modern monitoring platforms often integrate with security information and event management systems to correlate database events with broader system behavior. This supports compliance with regulatory standards such as GDPR, HIPAA, and PCI-DSS, which require strict access control, data protection, and audit logging policies. By centralizing and analyzing these security metrics, organizations can build more resilient and trustworthy data infrastructures.

Monitoring must also account for the evolving nature of databases. As systems adopt microservices architectures, containerization, and serverless technologies, traditional monitoring techniques may no longer suffice. Observability platforms must adapt to ephemeral workloads, autoscaling environments, and dynamically provisioned storage. Exporting metrics in standard formats, supporting open telemetry protocols, and integrating with cloud-native tools is essential to maintain visibility in modern environments. Monitoring should not be an afterthought but a first-class design consideration, embedded in the architecture from the outset.

A successful monitoring strategy includes not just the tools and metrics but also the people and processes to act on them. Alerts must be routed to the appropriate responders, supported by clear runbooks and incident workflows. Escalation policies, post-incident reviews, and continuous feedback loops ensure that monitoring drives improvement rather than merely reporting problems. Empowering teams to understand and use monitoring data fosters a culture of accountability and operational excellence.

Monitoring tools and metrics provide the insight required to maintain fast, reliable, and secure database systems. They enable early detection of problems, guide performance optimization efforts, support scalability, and uphold compliance. By continuously observing and analyzing key metrics, organizations can anticipate challenges, adapt to change, and deliver consistent service to users and stakeholders. In the increasingly complex and demanding world of data management, monitoring is not just a technical requirement but a strategic advantage.

Load Testing and Benchmarking

Load testing and benchmarking are fundamental practices in evaluating the performance, scalability, and reliability of database systems under real-world and extreme conditions. These practices simulate expected workloads and push systems to their operational limits to reveal potential weaknesses, capacity constraints, and performance bottlenecks. Understanding how a database behaves under various types of load is essential for making informed architectural decisions, optimizing resource allocation, and preparing for periods of high demand. Load testing and benchmarking are not isolated exercises performed during deployment but ongoing processes that guide continuous performance tuning and system refinement throughout the lifecycle of a database.

The purpose of load testing is to observe how a database responds when subjected to different levels of workload, which may include high volumes of concurrent users, simultaneous queries, write-intensive operations, or complex analytical computations. Load testing helps determine the upper limits of throughput, the stability of transactions under pressure, and the latency introduced as load increases. It also highlights whether performance degrades linearly, exponentially, or remains stable as workload increases. By applying controlled and incremental loads, administrators can identify performance thresholds and establish the maximum sustainable capacity of a system before it becomes unstable or unresponsive.

Benchmarking, in contrast, involves measuring specific performance metrics under defined conditions to compare different systems, configurations, or optimization strategies. Benchmarking allows organizations to quantify improvements, validate changes, and make data-driven decisions. Standardized benchmarks such as TPC-C and TPC-H provide widely accepted methods for evaluating transactional and analytical performance respectively. However, custom benchmarks tailored to the organization's specific workload patterns are often more informative and actionable. These benchmarks include simulated user behavior, realistic query mixes, and replication of production data models to ensure that the results reflect actual system use.

A critical aspect of both load testing and benchmarking is the preparation of a representative environment. Tests conducted on isolated or artificially simplified environments may produce misleading results. Ideally, the testing environment should mirror the production system as closely as possible, including the same hardware specifications, network topology, database configurations, and data volumes. When exact replication is not feasible, the environment should at least scale proportionally to the real system. Synthetic data used in testing must also mimic the distribution, cardinality, and relationships of real data to ensure that query execution paths and indexing behaviors are realistic.

Test design is another vital component. Load tests must be carefully constructed to include a balanced mix of read and write operations, varied query complexities, and different transaction types. Including operations such as inserts, updates, deletes, joins, aggregations, and stored procedure calls ensures that all aspects of the system are exercised. Timing patterns must reflect expected user behavior, including bursts of activity, sustained load, and idle periods. Tests must run long enough to capture the effects of caching, memory saturation, and background processes such as garbage collection or index maintenance. For systems with periodic jobs, such as data loading or backups, these activities should be included in the testing schedule to measure their impact on performance.

Metrics collection during testing is essential for interpretation and analysis. Key metrics include query latency, transactions per second, CPU and memory utilization, disk I/O, lock contention, and network throughput. These metrics provide a multi-dimensional view of how the system responds under pressure. More granular data, such as execution plans, wait events, and session statistics, helps pinpoint specific causes of degradation. Visualization tools, dashboards, and logs help aggregate and interpret the data, making it easier to draw meaningful conclusions and identify areas for improvement.

One of the primary goals of load testing is to detect performance bottlenecks. Bottlenecks may appear in different layers of the system, including the application logic, database engine, operating system, or underlying hardware. For example, high CPU usage may indicate inefficient queries or suboptimal indexing, while high I/O wait times may point to storage latency or insufficient memory. Lock contention and concurrency issues often become evident only under load, revealing problems with transaction isolation or access patterns. Addressing these bottlenecks often requires collaboration between database administrators, developers, and system architects to implement fixes that span multiple components.

Benchmarking can also be used to evaluate the impact of changes, such as a new database version, hardware upgrade, or configuration adjustment. By establishing a performance baseline and comparing it to post-change results, organizations can verify that the change achieved its intended effect without introducing regressions. Benchmarking is particularly useful in evaluating alternative database engines or architectures, such as transitioning from a monolithic system to a distributed database, or from on-premises hosting to a cloud platform. Objective performance comparisons help guide strategic decisions and avoid costly missteps.

Load testing and benchmarking play an essential role in capacity planning. By understanding how a system performs under load, administrators can predict when resources will be exhausted and plan for scaling accordingly. This planning includes provisioning additional CPU, memory, or storage, adding read replicas, partitioning data, or implementing caching strategies. In cloud environments, auto-scaling mechanisms can be fine-tuned based on empirical data gathered during tests. Predictive modeling based on benchmark results allows teams to forecast system behavior under future growth scenarios and design infrastructure that scales gracefully.

Test automation is increasingly important in managing the complexity and frequency of performance tests. Automated test suites can run scheduled benchmarks, simulate user load, and compare results against historical baselines. Integration with continuous integration and deployment pipelines ensures that performance regressions are detected early in the development cycle. Automated alerts, trend analysis, and anomaly detection reduce the need for manual oversight and enable faster response to emerging issues. Automation also supports more frequent testing, allowing organizations to maintain high performance standards as systems evolve.

While performance testing is often viewed as a technical activity, it has strategic implications across the organization. The results of load tests and benchmarks influence budget decisions, service level agreements, and customer satisfaction. They inform risk assessments, compliance audits, and disaster recovery plans. Communicating performance findings in a clear and actionable manner helps stakeholders understand the trade-offs involved in architectural decisions and reinforces the value of proactive performance management.

Load testing and benchmarking are not optional luxuries but essential disciplines for building robust, scalable, and high-performing database systems. They reveal how systems behave under stress, validate improvements, and guide planning for the future. By adopting rigorous testing methodologies, investing in realistic test environments, and committing to continuous measurement, organizations gain the confidence and clarity needed to support growing workloads, meet performance expectations, and deliver reliable services to users at scale.

Archiving Strategies for Cold Data

Archiving strategies for cold data are essential for maintaining the performance, manageability, and cost efficiency of modern database systems. As organizations generate and accumulate vast volumes of information, not all data remains equally important or frequently accessed. Over time, a significant portion of the data becomes cold, meaning it is infrequently used but must still be retained for historical reference, compliance, or business continuity. Without a structured approach to identifying, managing, and storing cold data, databases can become bloated, query performance may degrade, and infrastructure costs may rise unnecessarily. Implementing intelligent archiving strategies allows organizations to balance data availability with storage efficiency, ensuring that hot, warm, and cold data are handled according to their operational value.

Cold data archiving begins with the process of classification. Before data can be archived, it must be identified based on access patterns, modification frequency, and business relevance. This often involves analyzing logs, access histories, and data timestamps to determine which tables, partitions, or rows have not been queried or updated within a defined period. Criteria for identifying cold data vary depending on the industry, data type, and regulatory environment. In a financial system, transactions older than a year may be considered cold, whereas in a medical database, patient records may remain active for a much longer time. Proper classification ensures that only genuinely inactive data is targeted for archiving, avoiding disruptions to operational processes or analytical reporting.

Once cold data is identified, organizations must decide where and how to store it. One common approach is to move cold data to separate archival tables or databases within the same environment. This logical separation reduces the size of active datasets, improving the performance of indexes, queries, and maintenance tasks. For example, an e-commerce platform might archive completed orders that are more than two years old, storing them in a dedicated archive schema. This allows the primary order table to remain lean and optimized for recent transactions, while still providing access to historical data when needed. Archived tables can be indexed differently, compressed for space savings, and subjected to less frequent backup cycles, further reducing overhead.

Another approach involves physically relocating cold data to lower-cost storage tiers, such as network-attached storage, cloud-based object stores, or specialized archival systems. In cloud environments, services like Amazon S3 Glacier, Azure Archive Storage, or Google Cloud Archive offer cost-effective solutions for storing large volumes of rarely accessed data. These platforms provide long-term durability and compliance capabilities while minimizing storage expenses. However, retrieving data from these services can introduce latency, so they are best suited for data that is unlikely to be accessed frequently. Policies should be established to govern retrieval times, cost implications, and use cases that justify accessing archived data.

In systems where regulatory requirements dictate data retention periods, archiving strategies must include retention policies that align with legal mandates. These policies specify how long different categories of data must be retained, when they may be archived, and when they must be purged. For example, tax records may need to be kept for seven years, while user activity logs might be retained for only one year. Archiving strategies must include mechanisms for enforcing these policies, such as scheduled jobs that move data to archival storage after the required period and securely delete it once retention requirements expire. Automated lifecycle management tools can assist in implementing these processes, reducing manual effort and minimizing the risk of non-compliance.

Security and access control are critical components of any archiving strategy. Cold data may still contain sensitive or confidential information, including personally identifiable information, financial details, or proprietary business records. Archived data must be encrypted both in transit and at rest, and access should be restricted to authorized personnel only. Role-based access control, audit logging, and integration with identity management systems ensure that archived data is protected and access is traceable. Additionally, when archived data is stored in the cloud, organizations must ensure that the chosen provider complies with relevant data protection regulations and contractual obligations.

Performance considerations also influence archiving strategies. While the primary goal is to reduce the load on active systems, archived data must remain retrievable within acceptable timeframes. Some organizations implement hybrid strategies where cold data is retained in compressed formats on slower but still directly accessible storage, enabling it to be queried without full restoration. Others maintain metadata indexes that point to archived data, allowing users to search summaries or references without scanning the full archive. For analytics use cases, historical data may be periodically reloaded into staging environments for reporting purposes, ensuring that insights can still be derived from cold data without impacting production systems.

Documentation and traceability of archived data are essential for long-term manageability. As data is moved across systems and storage layers, maintaining metadata that describes the origin, structure, and context of the archived data ensures it can be interpreted correctly in the future. This includes schema definitions, data dictionaries, archive dates, and any transformations applied during archiving. Proper documentation supports audits, facilitates recovery, and ensures that future users or systems can access and understand the data without requiring tribal knowledge or legacy dependencies.

In data warehouses and big data environments, archiving strategies often involve data partitioning and tiered storage. Time-based partitioning allows older partitions to be stored on slower disks or offloaded to separate clusters, while newer partitions remain on high-speed storage for immediate access. Tiered storage systems automatically move data between performance and archival layers based on access frequency, optimizing both cost and speed. These strategies require coordination between database configurations, storage policies, and monitoring tools to function effectively and transparently.

Monitoring and auditing of archived data processes are vital for ensuring the reliability and integrity of the archiving system. Logging every archival operation, including what data was moved, when, where, and by whom, provides a verifiable trail that supports compliance and troubleshooting. Scheduled integrity checks, such as hash verifications or sample restorations, confirm that archived data remains intact and retrievable. Any failures in the archival process must trigger alerts and be subject to incident response procedures.

Cold data archiving is not simply a storage optimization exercise but a strategic element of data lifecycle management. It supports performance tuning, cost control, regulatory compliance, and long-term data governance. Implementing effective archiving strategies requires collaboration between database administrators, compliance officers, storage engineers, and business stakeholders. With a thoughtful approach, organizations can ensure that data remains accessible, secure, and usable across its entire lifecycle, from creation to archival and eventual disposal. In a world of exponential data growth, cold data archiving is a cornerstone of sustainable and intelligent information management.

Auditing and Compliance Considerations

Auditing and compliance considerations play a critical role in modern database management, especially in industries where sensitive data is collected, processed, stored, and shared. As regulatory frameworks grow increasingly stringent and data privacy becomes a central concern for consumers and organizations alike, the ability to demonstrate transparency, accountability, and data stewardship is no longer optional. It is an operational necessity. Auditing refers to the process of systematically recording and examining database activity to ensure that all actions are traceable and verifiable. Compliance, on the other hand, involves adhering to specific legal, contractual, and organizational requirements related to data handling and security. Together, these domains intersect to support risk management, regulatory obligations, and ethical data governance.

The foundation of a strong auditing strategy begins with understanding what activities need to be monitored and recorded. In database systems, this typically includes user logins, data access, query executions, modifications to data, schema changes, and administrative operations such as backups, configuration changes, and permission adjustments. These events are critical because they reveal who did what, when, and how. A complete audit trail enables organizations to reconstruct historical activity, investigate suspicious behavior, and ensure accountability among users and administrators. Effective auditing is not about surveillance but about establishing a trusted and verifiable record of events that reinforces system integrity and user confidence.

To meet compliance requirements, audit logs must be tamper-evident and securely stored. This means they should be protected from unauthorized access, modification, or deletion. Encryption at rest ensures that logs are secure even if the storage medium is compromised, while access controls and role-based privileges restrict who can view or manage logs. In some cases, organizations are required to retain logs for specific periods, ranging from a few months to several years, depending on the applicable regulations. For example, financial institutions subject to the Sarbanes-Oxley Act may need to preserve records for seven years, while healthcare providers under HIPAA must retain audit logs for six years. Automating log retention, archival, and purging helps enforce these policies and reduces administrative overhead.

Audit mechanisms can be implemented at different layers of the database stack. Native auditing features provided by relational database management systems offer deep visibility into internal operations. Oracle Database, Microsoft SQL Server, PostgreSQL, and MySQL all support built-in auditing capabilities that can be configured to track specific events or users. These features often integrate with system-wide logging solutions or security information and event management platforms. Alternatively, external tools and agents can capture database activity by monitoring network traffic, application logs, or system processes. While less invasive, these methods may lack the precision and completeness of native auditing but can serve as valuable supplements in distributed or heterogeneous environments.

The scope of compliance extends beyond internal policies and includes external regulations that dictate how data must be protected, accessed, and reported. Common frameworks include the General Data Protection Regulation in the European Union, the Health Insurance Portability and Accountability Act in the United States, the Payment Card Industry Data Security Standard for financial transactions, and the Federal Risk and Authorization Management Program for cloud service providers. These regulations impose strict rules around data minimization, consent, breach notification, cross-border transfers, and user rights such as data access and erasure. Compliance is not a checkbox but an ongoing commitment that requires continuous monitoring, periodic audits, and regular updates to policies and technologies.

Auditing is also critical for detecting and responding to security incidents. By analyzing audit logs, security teams can identify patterns that suggest unauthorized access, privilege escalation, or malicious activity. For instance, a sudden spike in failed login attempts, data exports outside business hours, or schema changes initiated by non-administrative users may indicate an ongoing attack or policy violation. Integrating audit logs with real-time alerting systems enables faster incident detection and response. Furthermore, retaining comprehensive audit trails supports forensic investigations, allowing organizations to trace the full scope of an incident and implement corrective measures.

Compliance also involves maintaining documentation and evidence that demonstrate adherence to standards. This includes policies on data access, user provisioning, data retention, encryption, and disaster recovery. Auditors may request records of who has access to specific data, when access was granted or revoked, and whether periodic reviews are conducted to validate permissions. Maintaining up-to-date documentation and automating compliance reporting streamlines the audit process and reduces the risk of non-compliance penalties. Self-assessments, third-party audits, and certification programs help validate that systems meet applicable standards and best practices.

One of the major challenges in auditing and compliance is balancing transparency with performance and privacy. Excessive auditing can introduce system overhead, consume storage, and degrade performance, especially in high-transaction environments. Selective auditing strategies that focus on high-risk activities or sensitive datasets help mitigate this impact while preserving the depth and value of audit data. On the privacy front, organizations must ensure that audit logs themselves do not become a source of sensitive data exposure. Logging tools must be configured to avoid capturing confidential information such as passwords, personal identifiers, or unencrypted records. When personal data is logged, access to logs must be tightly controlled, and logs must be subject to the same privacy protections as the primary data.

Modern cloud platforms offer specialized tools and services to support auditing and compliance. Services such as AWS CloudTrail, Azure Monitor, and Google Cloud Audit Logs provide centralized, scalable logging infrastructures that integrate with broader cloud security frameworks. These tools offer features like immutable logs, long-term archival, and advanced search capabilities, making it easier to detect anomalies and respond to compliance inquiries. Cloud-native databases also support fine-grained access controls and audit policies that align with multi-tenant environments and elastic workloads. Leveraging these capabilities requires careful configuration and ongoing oversight to ensure that policies keep pace with changing workloads, user roles, and compliance requirements.

Training and awareness are vital components of a successful auditing and compliance strategy. Users, developers, and administrators must understand their responsibilities regarding data access, security policies, and audit procedures. Regular training sessions, compliance briefings, and ethical use guidelines reinforce a culture of accountability and ensure that everyone is aligned with organizational standards. Encouraging responsible behavior, reporting of policy violations, and participation in internal audits helps embed compliance into the organizational fabric rather than treating it as a separate function.

Auditing and compliance considerations are inseparable from the overall health, security, and trustworthiness of a database system. They provide the controls and assurances that modern organizations need to operate in regulated environments and build confidence among stakeholders. Through careful planning, robust tooling, and a commitment to transparency, organizations can implement effective audit practices that uphold compliance, support security, and contribute to responsible data stewardship.

Security Implications of Backup and Indexing

The processes of backing up data and creating indexes are essential to the operation and performance of modern database systems, but they also introduce a wide range of security implications that must be carefully managed. These operations, while routine from a database administration perspective, can become weak points in an otherwise secure system if not properly protected. Backups represent complete or partial copies of critical data and are often targeted by malicious actors because they may contain unencrypted or inadequately protected sensitive information. Indexes, while improving performance, can also inadvertently expose sensitive attributes, making them a potential source of data leakage. Understanding and mitigating the security implications of backup and indexing is a crucial responsibility for any organization that values the integrity, confidentiality, and availability of its data.

Backups are often considered the last line of defense in data protection, particularly in scenarios involving data loss, corruption, or ransomware attacks. However, the very nature of backups makes them a high-value target. A backup file may contain user credentials, financial records, personally identifiable information, proprietary business data, or system configurations. If these files are not properly secured, an attacker who gains access to them can bypass many of the security controls in place within the live system. This is especially dangerous when backup files are stored in unsecured locations, transmitted without encryption, or retained beyond their useful life. Organizations must enforce strict policies around who can access backup files, how long they are retained, and where they are stored.

Encryption plays a central role in securing backups. Backup files must be encrypted both in transit and at rest to prevent unauthorized access. This means using secure transfer protocols such as TLS when sending backup files over networks and applying strong encryption algorithms to protect stored backup files on disk. Encryption keys must be managed securely through key management systems that enforce rotation, access controls, and audit trails. Without proper key management, even encrypted backups may be vulnerable if keys are stored in plaintext or accessible by unauthorized users. It is also important to test that encrypted backups can be decrypted reliably during restoration, as key loss can render data permanently inaccessible.

Access control mechanisms must be extended to backup systems with the same rigor applied to production data. Only authorized personnel should be able to initiate, modify, restore, or delete backups. Role-based access control should be implemented to ensure that different users have only the permissions required for their responsibilities. Backup logs and audit trails should be maintained to track all interactions with backup systems, including successful and failed access attempts. These logs can help identify malicious behavior, such as unauthorized data extraction or attempts to tamper with backup files, and they provide evidence for post-incident investigations.

Backups stored offsite or in the cloud require special attention. Cloud-based backup solutions offer scalability and convenience, but they must be configured carefully to avoid exposing data through misconfigured storage buckets, excessive permissions, or unpatched vulnerabilities. Cloud storage accounts must be protected with multi-factor authentication, network access restrictions, and encryption at the service level. Public access to backup locations must be strictly prohibited. Additionally, organizations should monitor cloud backup repositories for unusual activity, such as sudden spikes in downloads or access from unfamiliar locations. These could be early signs of compromise and require immediate investigation.

Indexing, while not typically associated with security, also carries risks that are often overlooked. Indexes can store copies of sensitive data fields, such as social security numbers, email addresses, or credit card numbers, depending on how they are created. This duplication means that sensitive data may reside in more than one location within the database, and each of those locations must be secured accordingly. A breach that exposes index files can lead to data leakage even if access to the main table is restricted. To mitigate this, indexes should be created only on columns that are necessary for performance optimization, and sensitive data should be excluded from indexing unless absolutely required. When sensitive data must be indexed, tokenization or hashing techniques may be used to obscure the original values.

Another security concern related to indexing is information inference. Indexes improve query performance by revealing which values exist in the underlying dataset and where they are located. If a user can issue queries against an index or deduce index contents through timing attacks or error messages, they may be able to infer the presence or absence of specific values, even without direct access to the data. This risk is particularly pronounced in multi-tenant environments where users must be strictly isolated from each other. Limiting metadata exposure, controlling query feedback, and restricting access to index statistics can help reduce the potential for inference-based attacks.

Index maintenance operations, such as rebuilds or reorganizations, can also impact security. These operations may temporarily expose unencrypted data in memory, on disk, or in logs, especially if diagnostic tools or debug modes are enabled during the process. Database administrators must ensure that index maintenance is performed securely, with encryption and access controls in place, and that temporary files are securely deleted afterward. It is also important to verify that index rebuilds do not inadvertently increase permissions or visibility for sensitive data through the creation of new execution plans or access paths.

Both backup and indexing strategies must be included in the organization's broader data governance and security frameworks. This includes regular security assessments, penetration testing, and vulnerability scanning of backup infrastructure and indexing configurations. Security policies must be documented, communicated, and enforced consistently across all teams involved in data management. Training and awareness programs should educate personnel about the specific risks associated with backups and indexes and the best practices for mitigating them. Automation tools can help enforce security policies by monitoring compliance, flagging misconfigurations, and alerting administrators to deviations from standard procedures.

The intersection of backup and indexing with security is complex and multi-faceted. These processes touch nearly every part of the data lifecycle and must be managed with the same attention to detail as primary security measures like authentication, firewalling, and intrusion detection. As threat actors become more sophisticated and data volumes continue to grow, the importance of securing every aspect of data handling, including backups and indexes, becomes increasingly clear. By addressing these risks proactively and comprehensively, organizations can protect their data assets, maintain trust with users and regulators, and ensure the long-term resilience of their information systems.

Encryption and Secure Data Handling

Encryption and secure data handling are fundamental components of modern database management practices, especially in environments where data confidentiality, integrity, and regulatory compliance are critical. As the volume and sensitivity of stored data continue to increase across industries, so too do the risks associated with unauthorized access, data breaches, and internal misuse. Encryption serves as a powerful safeguard, rendering data unreadable to unauthorized users, while secure data handling encompasses a broad set of practices that ensure data is protected throughout its lifecycle. Together, these disciplines form the backbone of a resilient security posture that can adapt to evolving threats and regulatory demands.

Encryption involves the transformation of plaintext data into an unreadable format using cryptographic algorithms. Only authorized users with the appropriate decryption keys can convert the data back into its original form. There are two primary types of encryption used in database systems: encryption at rest and encryption in transit. Encryption at rest protects data stored on disk, including databases, logs, and backup files. This ensures that even if storage devices are physically stolen or accessed without authorization, the data remains protected. Encryption in transit secures data as it moves across networks, preventing interception or tampering during communication between clients, applications, and databases. Both forms of encryption are essential for comprehensive protection.

The strength of encryption relies not only on the algorithm used but also on how encryption keys are generated, stored, and managed. Key management systems are critical to ensuring that encryption keys are kept secure and accessible only to authorized entities. Keys should be rotated regularly, stored separately from encrypted data, and protected by access controls, auditing, and tamper-evident mechanisms. If encryption keys are lost or compromised, data may become irretrievable or vulnerable. Organizations must implement policies and procedures for key generation, distribution, rotation, revocation, and recovery. These practices ensure that encryption remains an effective line of defense rather than a potential point of failure.

In addition to full-database encryption, many systems support column-level or field-level encryption. This allows specific sensitive attributes such as social security numbers, credit card data, or health records to be encrypted while leaving non-sensitive fields in plaintext for efficient processing. Field-level encryption provides fine-grained control over data confidentiality and is especially useful when only a subset of the data needs protection. However, this approach adds complexity to query logic and indexing, as encrypted fields are typically not searchable or sortable without additional mechanisms like deterministic encryption or specialized indexes. Designing secure yet usable encryption strategies requires balancing performance, functionality, and protection requirements.

Secure data handling encompasses all the procedures and controls associated with how data is created, stored, processed, accessed, and destroyed. It begins with data classification, where data is categorized based on sensitivity, value, and regulatory requirements. Data classified as sensitive or confidential must be handled with stricter controls, including access restrictions, encryption, and auditing. Proper classification ensures that security measures are applied proportionately and consistently, reducing the risk of overexposure or negligence. Data minimization is another principle of secure handling that involves collecting and retaining only the data necessary for a specific purpose. Minimizing data reduces the risk surface and helps organizations comply with data protection regulations that mandate limits on data retention and processing.

Access control is one of the most critical aspects of secure data handling. Only authorized users and applications should be allowed to access or modify sensitive data. This is enforced through authentication mechanisms such as passwords, tokens, certificates, and multi-factor authentication. Authorization policies define what actions each user or role is permitted to perform. Fine-grained access control ensures that users only see or modify the data they are explicitly allowed to handle, reducing the risk of privilege abuse or accidental exposure. Role-based access control simplifies administration by assigning permissions to roles instead of individual users, while attribute-based access control offers more dynamic and context-aware enforcement.

Monitoring and auditing are essential components of both encryption and secure handling strategies. Every access to sensitive data should be logged and reviewed to detect anomalies, enforce accountability, and support forensic investigations. Audit logs should record who accessed what data, when, and from where, along with any changes made. These logs must be protected from tampering and integrated into centralized monitoring systems that can trigger alerts when suspicious activity is detected. Regular audits of access privileges, encryption configurations, and data flows help maintain a consistent security posture and ensure compliance with internal policies and external regulations.

Data masking is another technique used in secure data handling, particularly in non-production environments. Masking replaces sensitive data with realistic but fictitious values, allowing developers and analysts to work with representative datasets without exposing real information. Static data masking alters data at rest, while dynamic masking modifies data on the fly during queries. This approach is valuable in test, development, and training environments where the use of live production data is unnecessary or unsafe. Effective data masking reduces the risk of exposure while preserving the usability of datasets for legitimate purposes.

Secure disposal of data is the final phase of the data lifecycle and must be handled with care to prevent residual data from being recovered. Simply deleting files or records is insufficient, as deleted data can often be restored with basic tools. Secure disposal methods include overwriting data multiple times, using cryptographic erasure, or physically destroying storage media. When data is archived, encryption helps ensure that even if storage media becomes obsolete or is lost, the data remains protected. Organizations should implement data retention and deletion policies that specify when and how data is to be securely removed based on classification and regulatory mandates.

In cloud and hybrid environments, encryption and secure data handling become even more critical due to the shared responsibility model. While cloud providers offer infrastructure-level security controls, customers remain responsible for securing their own data. This includes configuring encryption settings, managing keys, setting up access policies, and ensuring secure data flows between on-premises and cloud systems. Cloud-native services often provide integrated tools for encryption, access control, and compliance management, but misconfiguration remains a leading cause of data exposure. Organizations must apply rigorous governance, monitor cloud configurations, and conduct regular risk assessments to maintain secure data handling practices across environments.

Encryption and secure data handling are not static checkboxes but continuous practices that evolve alongside threats, technologies, and regulations. They require collaboration among database administrators, security teams, developers, compliance officers, and business leaders. A comprehensive security framework includes not just tools and technologies but also training, awareness, and a culture of responsibility. By embedding encryption and secure handling into every stage of data management, organizations can protect sensitive information, earn customer trust, and confidently navigate the complexities of a digital world.

Data Retention Policies and Governance

Data retention policies and governance are essential elements of modern information management practices. In an era where organizations collect vast quantities of data across various systems and departments, it is no longer feasible to store everything indefinitely without consequence. Data that is not governed effectively can become a liability, increasing the risk of breaches, regulatory violations, inefficiencies, and rising storage costs. A well-designed data retention policy defines how long data should be stored, when it should be archived, and when it must be securely deleted. Governance, on the other hand, ensures that these policies are consistently enforced, monitored, and aligned with business, legal, and regulatory requirements.

The purpose of a data retention policy is to provide a structured framework that balances data availability with legal, operational, and compliance needs. Not all data holds the same value over time. Some information is required for short-term transactional use, while other types must be retained for years to meet financial auditing, legal discovery, or regulatory obligations. Retention policies define specific timeframes for each category of data based on classification, sensitivity, usage, and origin. For example, tax records may need to be retained for seven years in some jurisdictions, while personnel files might be kept for the duration of employment plus an additional retention period. Without a clearly defined policy, organizations face the risk of holding data longer than necessary or deleting it too early, either of which can result in serious consequences.

A foundational aspect of data retention governance is data classification. This involves assigning categories to data based on its type, sensitivity, and business value. Categories may include public, internal, confidential, and regulated data, each with corresponding handling and retention rules. Classification enables organizations to apply targeted retention periods and security controls, reducing the complexity and risks associated with managing unstructured or undocumented information. Once classified, data governance teams can map data flows, identify storage locations, and ensure that policies are enforced consistently across systems and repositories.

Technology plays a critical role in enforcing data retention policies. Automated tools can monitor file creation and modification dates, trigger alerts when data approaches its retention threshold, and initiate archival or deletion processes when appropriate. Database systems, enterprise content management platforms, and data warehouses often include lifecycle management features that support retention enforcement. These tools must be configured correctly to avoid accidental deletion or policy violations. For example, automated scripts may archive customer transaction data after a certain period while retaining only summaries for reporting purposes. Similarly, email systems may implement retention tags that dictate how long messages are stored before being purged or archived.

Legal and regulatory compliance is one of the strongest drivers for implementing robust data retention governance. Organizations across sectors must comply with a growing number of regulations such as the General Data Protection Regulation in Europe, the California Consumer Privacy Act, the Health Insurance Portability and Accountability Act, and industry-specific requirements like FINRA or SEC rules for financial institutions. These regulations often mandate minimum or maximum retention periods, data subject rights such as the right to be forgotten, and documentation requirements that prove compliance efforts. Failure to meet these obligations can result in significant penalties, reputational damage, and legal disputes. By codifying retention policies into enforceable governance frameworks, organizations can demonstrate due diligence and readiness for audits or investigations.

Retention policies must also account for the lifecycle of data from creation through archiving to secure disposal. Retention is not just about keeping data for a certain period but about ensuring that it is handled appropriately throughout its existence. During the active phase, data is typically stored in high-performance systems where it supports business processes and is frequently accessed. As it becomes less relevant, data may be moved to archival systems that offer lower cost storage but slower retrieval speeds. Finally, at the end of its lifecycle, data must be securely deleted or anonymized to prevent unauthorized access or misuse. Governance must include procedures for each of these transitions, including verification steps, audit logging, and exception handling for records under legal hold or litigation.

Governance also encompasses the assignment of responsibility for data retention within the organization. Clear ownership is necessary to ensure accountability and consistency. Data stewards, compliance officers, legal counsel, and IT administrators must work together to define and implement policies. Business units that generate or consume data must be involved in determining what information is needed, how long it remains relevant, and how retention rules affect operations. Communication and training are key elements of governance, ensuring that employees understand their roles, follow procedures, and report anomalies or policy violations. Periodic reviews and policy updates are also essential to reflect changes in regulations, business practices, or technology.

Retention policies must be adaptable to different data types and storage formats. Structured data in relational databases, unstructured data in file systems, logs from applications, backups, and metadata all require different handling approaches. Some data may be embedded in legacy systems that do not support automated retention, requiring manual oversight or migration. Others may reside in third-party platforms or cloud environments, where service-level agreements must align with organizational retention policies. Governance must ensure that policies are applied uniformly, regardless of data location, and that external vendors are contractually obligated to comply with retention requirements.

Another important consideration is the relationship between retention and security. Data that is retained beyond its useful life increases the potential impact of a breach. Threat actors often target old data because it is less protected, less monitored, and often overlooked during security planning. Reducing the volume of retained data minimizes the risk of exposure, simplifies compliance audits, and improves system performance. Governance teams must evaluate not only how long data is kept but also how securely it is stored, who has access, and how frequently it is reviewed. Retention policies should include encryption requirements, access control standards, and audit logging to support both privacy and security goals.

Data retention policies and governance frameworks are essential to responsible data stewardship in today's information-driven economy. They provide the structure and controls necessary to manage data growth, ensure legal compliance, protect privacy, and reduce risk. Through classification, automation, collaboration, and continuous oversight, organizations can turn data retention from a reactive burden into a proactive strategy that supports operational efficiency, regulatory compliance, and long-term business value. As data continues to expand across platforms, devices, and jurisdictions, the importance of disciplined, well-governed retention practices will only continue to grow.

NoSQL Indexing Models

NoSQL databases have emerged as powerful alternatives to traditional relational systems, particularly in applications that demand scalability, flexibility, and high availability. With their schema-less architectures and distributed nature, NoSQL databases are well-suited for managing large volumes of unstructured or semi-structured data. However, the absence of rigid schemas and structured relations introduces new challenges in how data is indexed and queried efficiently. Indexing in NoSQL systems is fundamentally different from that in relational databases, often tailored to the specific characteristics of the underlying data model, such as document, key-value, wide-column, or graph structures. Understanding how NoSQL indexing models function is critical to designing performant systems that can meet diverse application requirements without sacrificing speed or reliability.

In document-oriented databases like MongoDB and Couchbase, data is stored in JSON or BSON format as documents, each potentially containing deeply nested fields and varying structures. Indexing in these systems is crucial because queries often target specific fields within documents rather than the document as a whole. The most common indexing mechanism is the single-field index, which allows rapid lookup based on the value of one field. These indexes are typically implemented as B-tree structures and enable efficient filtering and sorting. In addition to single-field indexes, compound indexes support queries that filter on multiple fields. However, developers must carefully consider the order of fields in compound indexes, as it affects which queries can leverage the index. For instance, an index on fields A and B can efficiently serve queries on A alone or A and B together, but not B alone.

Document databases also support multikey indexes, which are used when indexing array values. These indexes create separate index entries for each element of an array field, allowing efficient querying over arrays. For example, if a document has a field that stores a list of tags, a multikey index can facilitate fast searches for documents containing a specific tag. The complexity increases when combined with compound indexes, as developers must ensure that multikey indexing does not introduce performance penalties due to excessive index size or duplication. Another advanced option is the text index, which supports full-text search within string fields. This is particularly useful for applications like content management systems, where users need to search large volumes of textual content based on keywords, stemming, or relevance scoring.

In key-value stores such as Redis or Amazon DynamoDB, indexing is inherently tied to how keys are managed. These systems offer high-speed access by key, making them ideal for use cases like caching, session storage, or real-time analytics. However, indexing beyond the primary key requires additional mechanisms. For example, DynamoDB allows the creation of secondary indexes, including global secondary indexes and local secondary indexes. Global secondary indexes support querying on any attribute, independent of the primary key, while local secondary indexes maintain a fixed partition key but allow queries on alternate sort keys. These indexes must be designed thoughtfully, as they incur additional storage and write costs. Since NoSQL systems often favor write availability and speed, maintaining secondary indexes can affect write throughput and consistency, especially in distributed environments.

Wide-column databases like Apache Cassandra or HBase organize data into rows and dynamic columns grouped into column families. Primary access in these systems is based on a combination of partition keys and clustering keys, forming a composite primary key. Indexing in wide-column stores relies heavily on the design of these keys, which determine how data is partitioned and sorted across the cluster. In Cassandra, for example, data is automatically indexed by the primary key, but additional secondary indexes can be defined on non-key columns. However, secondary indexes in Cassandra are not globally distributed and may perform poorly on high-cardinality attributes or in scenarios with frequent updates. As a result, developers often denormalize data or create manual indexing tables that map attribute values to their corresponding primary keys, effectively simulating inverted indexes.

In graph databases like Neo4j or Amazon Neptune, data is modeled as nodes, relationships, and properties. Indexing in graph databases is primarily used to find starting points for graph traversals. Property indexes on nodes or relationships enable fast lookup of entities with specific attributes, such as a person with a given name or a product with a certain category. Once a starting point is identified, graph algorithms or traversal queries follow edges to explore related entities. This differs from traditional indexing in that the performance of a query depends more on the efficiency of traversal algorithms and the structure of the graph than on the index alone. Some graph databases support full-text search indexes or spatial indexes to enhance query capabilities. Indexing strategies in this context must be aligned with traversal patterns and query complexity to avoid excessive memory usage or long response times.

Across all NoSQL models, indexing must be aligned with the anticipated access patterns of the application. Because NoSQL systems typically avoid expensive operations like joins or cross-partition scans, indexes must be designed to support efficient retrieval of all necessary data in a single query. This often leads to denormalization, where data is duplicated across multiple documents or records to optimize read performance. While this reduces the need for complex joins, it increases the importance of indexing to avoid excessive scanning or filtering. Developers must also account for eventual consistency models, which can affect the visibility of newly indexed data. Index updates may lag behind writes in some distributed systems, leading to temporary inconsistencies in query results.

Index maintenance is another critical consideration. As data is inserted, updated, or deleted, indexes must be updated accordingly. In high-write environments, this can become a performance bottleneck. Some NoSQL systems offer options to disable indexing temporarily during bulk operations or to defer index updates until a later point. Administrators must monitor index sizes, evaluate their impact on storage and I/O, and periodically rebuild or drop unused indexes to maintain optimal performance. Monitoring tools and query profilers provided by NoSQL platforms help assess index usage, identify slow queries, and suggest indexing improvements.

In conclusion, NoSQL indexing models reflect the diversity and specialization of the systems in which they operate. Unlike the relatively uniform B-tree indexes in relational databases, NoSQL indexing mechanisms vary widely depending on the data model, query capabilities, and scalability goals of the database. Developers must understand the indexing options available within their chosen platform and design indexes that support efficient data access while minimizing storage and maintenance overhead. The success of a NoSQL deployment depends not only on the flexibility and scalability of the database but also on the intelligence and foresight applied to indexing strategy.

Indexing in Columnar Databases

Indexing in columnar databases is a topic of significant importance, especially in the context of analytical workloads and data warehousing. Columnar databases, also known as column-oriented databases, store data by columns rather than rows, which allows for highly efficient compression, faster read performance for selective queries, and optimized operations for aggregations and scans. This storage paradigm fundamentally changes the way indexing is approached and implemented. Unlike traditional row-based databases that often rely heavily on B-tree and hash indexes to speed up individual row lookups, columnar databases leverage a different set of strategies tailored to their underlying architecture and query patterns.

The core advantage of columnar storage lies in the physical layout of data. Because each column is stored separately, queries that target specific columns can read only the data necessary for the operation, avoiding the overhead of fetching entire rows. This is particularly useful for analytical queries that aggregate values, filter based on columnar conditions, or retrieve a narrow slice of data across many records. In this context, indexing must complement the native efficiencies of the columnar format rather than duplicate or override them. This leads to the adoption of indexing techniques such as zone maps, bitmap indexes, and dictionary encoding, each of which is designed to work in harmony with columnar storage and access patterns.

Zone maps are one of the most commonly used indexing techniques in columnar databases. A zone map stores metadata about blocks of column values, typically the minimum and maximum value in a block. When a query with a filtering condition is executed, the database engine can quickly eliminate blocks where the value of interest cannot possibly reside. For example, if a block has values ranging from 100 to 200, and the query is searching for records with values less than 50, the entire block can be skipped. This form of coarse indexing is very effective in reducing the number of blocks read from disk, especially when data is sorted or exhibits natural clustering. The performance benefit is not from speeding up row retrieval but from avoiding unnecessary I/O operations.

Bitmap indexing is another powerful method employed in columnar databases. A bitmap index represents the distinct values in a column and maps each value to a bitmap where each bit corresponds to a row and indicates whether the value exists at that position. Bitmap indexes are particularly effective for columns with low cardinality, where the number of distinct values is relatively small. They enable very fast filtering and Boolean operations, such as AND, OR, and NOT, across multiple columns. For example, a query that filters by gender and country can use bitmap operations to quickly compute the set of matching rows without scanning the entire dataset. Because of the columnar layout, combining bitmaps is both memory-efficient and computationally fast, making bitmap indexing ideal for OLAP-style queries with multiple filter predicates.

Dictionary encoding is another native optimization that functions as a lightweight index in columnar databases. In this approach, unique column values are mapped to integer codes, and the column is stored as an array of these codes. The dictionary is stored alongside the column and is used during query processing to resolve values. This method reduces storage footprint and improves cache performance, as integer comparisons are faster than string comparisons. Although dictionary encoding is not a traditional index in the relational sense, it provides indexing-like benefits by enabling quick lookups and reducing the volume of data processed. Dictionary encoding also works well with compression algorithms, further enhancing the efficiency of columnar storage.

Some columnar databases support secondary indexing mechanisms that resemble those in row-oriented systems. These indexes are often optional and used to accelerate specific types of queries, such as point lookups or range scans on columns not sorted or clustered. However, because columnar systems are typically optimized for bulk reads rather than individual row access, secondary indexes are used sparingly. When they are implemented, they often combine elements of B-tree or skip list structures with the columnar format, allowing selective access to column values without compromising scan performance. These indexes must be carefully maintained and are best used in scenarios where specific access patterns justify their overhead.

Another important consideration in columnar indexing is data sorting. Columnar databases often benefit significantly from sorting data on load or during periodic maintenance. When data is sorted on one or more columns, filtering operations become more efficient, as the sorted structure aligns well with zone maps and binary search algorithms. Sorted data enhances compression by increasing value locality and improves the performance of queries that involve range predicates or ordered aggregations. In some systems, sorting can be a more effective performance optimization than indexing, particularly when the same columns are frequently used in filters or joins.

Index maintenance in columnar databases is generally less burdensome than in traditional systems because the columnar model itself supports efficient scanning and filtering. However, when explicit indexes are used, they must be kept in sync with data inserts, updates, and deletes. This can introduce overhead, especially in systems with high data volatility. For this reason, many columnar databases are optimized for append-only workloads, where data is ingested in batches and rarely modified. Index structures can then be rebuilt or merged periodically in the background, minimizing the impact on query performance. Systems like Amazon Redshift, Apache Parquet-based engines, and Vertica often employ background vacuuming and compaction processes to maintain data structures and indexes without manual intervention.

Columnar databases used in distributed environments face additional challenges and opportunities with indexing. Data may be sharded or partitioned across multiple nodes, and indexing strategies must account for distributed query execution. Indexes may be local to each shard or global across the cluster. Global indexing enables more powerful query optimizations but requires coordination and metadata synchronization. Local indexing is simpler and scales more easily but may result in less efficient global query plans. As with all aspects of distributed systems, trade-offs between consistency, availability, and performance influence how indexing is implemented and used.

Indexing in columnar databases is not about replicating the mechanisms of traditional relational systems but about leveraging the strengths of the columnar architecture. It requires a deep understanding of how data is stored, queried, and maintained. The choice of indexing strategy depends on data characteristics, workload patterns, and system capabilities. By selecting appropriate indexing techniques such as zone maps, bitmap indexes, and dictionary encoding, and by combining them with sorting and compression, organizations can build high-performance analytical platforms that deliver rapid insights across massive datasets. In this landscape, indexing is both a science and an art, integral to unlocking the full potential of columnar data systems.

Hybrid Storage Models and Optimization

Hybrid storage models have emerged as a practical and powerful approach to address the growing complexity of modern data management. As organizations accumulate increasingly diverse types of data—structured, semi-structured, and unstructured—and as workloads shift between transactional and analytical use cases, the limitations of relying on a single storage paradigm become evident. Hybrid storage models combine elements of row-oriented and column-oriented storage strategies, seeking to deliver the best of both worlds by optimizing for both high-performance transactional operations and fast analytical processing. The hybrid approach is particularly valuable in systems that serve mixed workloads or in architectures where operational data must be analyzed in real time without duplication or latency.

In a traditional row-oriented storage model, data is stored one row at a time, meaning that all columns of a row are physically co-located on disk. This format is ideal for transactional workloads where the primary access pattern involves reading or writing full rows. Operations such as inserting a new record, updating a specific user's information, or retrieving an order by ID benefit from this model because the entire row can be retrieved with a single I/O operation. However, when it comes to analytical queries that need to scan and aggregate large volumes of data across a few specific columns, row-based storage becomes inefficient due to the need to read irrelevant columns alongside the relevant ones.

In contrast, columnar storage organizes data by column, storing values from the same column together. This format excels at analytical queries because only the necessary columns are read, reducing I/O and enabling better compression due to the homogeneity of data types within columns. Aggregations, filters, and groupings are performed more efficiently, especially when combined with vectorized processing and advanced compression algorithms. Yet, for transactional use cases that involve frequent inserts, updates, or point queries on full rows, columnar storage may introduce latency due to the need to access multiple column files and reconstruct the row in memory.

Hybrid storage models aim to resolve this tension by integrating both row and column storage formats within a single system or architecture. There are several ways in which this integration can be implemented. One common method is to maintain dual-format storage, where data is simultaneously stored in both row-based and column-based formats.

This duality allows the system to choose the optimal format for a given query based on its access pattern. The challenge with this approach lies in maintaining consistency between the two formats, ensuring that updates are applied to both storage representations in a timely and efficient manner. Techniques such as change data capture, delta storage, and background synchronization are often employed to manage this consistency.

Another approach is to use a write-optimized row store for incoming data and a read-optimized column store for analytical queries, with periodic batch processes that transform and load data from the row store into the column store. This is commonly seen in systems that adopt a lambda architecture, where the speed layer handles real-time transactional data and the batch layer processes data for analytics. This separation allows each layer to be tuned independently, but introduces complexity in terms of data movement, duplication, and eventual consistency. Emerging architectures such as kappa and unified analytics frameworks seek to streamline this process by minimizing redundancy and enabling near real-time synchronization between transactional and analytical stores.

Some modern databases, often referred to as hybrid transactional and analytical processing systems or HTAP systems, are designed from the ground up to support hybrid storage and workload patterns. These systems dynamically determine the most efficient storage format for each table or partition based on usage statistics, query patterns, and data characteristics. For example, frequently updated data may remain in a row-based format, while historical or read-heavy data is migrated to columnar storage. Such adaptive storage strategies require sophisticated query planners and storage engines capable of managing heterogeneous data layouts and optimizing access paths accordingly. Systems like SAP HANA, Google BigQuery, and Microsoft Azure Synapse exemplify this trend by integrating in-memory, columnar, and disk-based storage technologies to support seamless hybrid workloads.

Optimization in hybrid storage models involves not just the choice of storage format, but also strategies for partitioning, indexing, caching, and data lifecycle management. Horizontal partitioning allows data to be split across multiple storage formats based on temporal, categorical, or usage-based criteria. For instance, recent data can be stored in a fast row-based cache for low-latency access, while older data is archived in a compressed columnar format for efficient analytical queries. Vertical partitioning splits tables by column groups, enabling sensitive or frequently accessed fields to be stored differently from large, infrequently used fields. These partitioning strategies must be supported by intelligent metadata management and query routing to ensure that the optimizer selects the correct storage location without introducing latency or inconsistency.

Caching plays a significant role in hybrid storage optimization. Frequently accessed data can be held in memory using row-oriented structures to accelerate point lookups and transactional updates. At the same time, columnar caches may be used to speed up repetitive analytical queries, especially those involving aggregations or filtering on popular columns. Caches must be kept coherent with the underlying data stores, requiring fine-grained invalidation and refresh mechanisms. In systems that support in-memory computing, hot data can be entirely resident in memory, enabling sub-second query performance for both transactional and analytical workloads.

Compression techniques also vary between row and column storage and can be selectively applied in hybrid models to maximize performance and reduce storage costs. Row-based compression typically uses record-level encoding and deduplication, while column-based compression benefits from techniques such as run-length encoding, dictionary encoding, and delta encoding. Hybrid systems often use a combination of these methods, applying the most appropriate compression scheme based on column cardinality, data type, and volatility.

Monitoring and tuning are critical in hybrid environments to ensure that storage strategies remain aligned with evolving workloads. Query logs, usage statistics, and performance metrics must be continuously analyzed to detect shifts in access patterns that might warrant rebalancing between row and column storage. Automated advisors and self-tuning systems can recommend or apply changes to storage formats, partitioning schemes, or indexing structures to maintain optimal performance. Governance and data quality tools must also be integrated to ensure that data integrity is preserved across multiple storage formats and that compliance requirements are consistently enforced.

Hybrid storage models represent a sophisticated evolution in database architecture, addressing the limitations of single-format storage through intelligent integration and optimization. By combining the strengths of row and column storage and dynamically adapting to changing workloads, hybrid models enable organizations to achieve high performance, scalability, and flexibility across a wide range of data-intensive applications. The careful design and optimization of hybrid storage systems are essential for unlocking the full potential of modern data platforms and delivering timely, actionable insights without compromise.

Schema Evolution and Migration Planning

Schema evolution and migration planning are critical aspects of maintaining the integrity, performance, and scalability of a database system over time. As business requirements change, applications evolve, and new features are introduced, the underlying database schema must adapt accordingly. This process, known as schema evolution, involves modifying the structure of database tables, relationships, constraints, and indexes without disrupting the availability or correctness of data. Migration planning, on the other hand, refers to the comprehensive set of strategies and procedures used to implement these changes safely and efficiently across different environments. Together, these practices ensure that database systems remain aligned with application logic and business objectives while minimizing risks associated with data loss, downtime, or degraded performance.

Schema changes are inevitable in any long-lived software system. They may include adding new columns to accommodate additional data, changing data types to support new formats, renaming columns or tables for clarity, splitting or merging tables to reflect changes in data modeling, or introducing new constraints and indexes to enforce business rules or improve performance. Each of these changes has the potential to impact application behavior, query execution plans, and data consistency. Therefore, schema evolution must be approached methodically, with careful consideration of backward compatibility, version control, and deployment coordination.

A fundamental principle in schema evolution is that changes should be backward-compatible whenever possible. This means that existing applications and queries should continue to function correctly after the schema is modified. For example, when adding a new column to a table, it is advisable to assign a default value or allow nulls to prevent errors in queries that do not reference the new column. Similarly, renaming or deleting columns should be avoided unless all dependent queries, stored procedures, and application code have been updated. Backward compatibility is especially important in environments where multiple application versions coexist or where deployments occur incrementally across distributed systems.

Version control for database schemas is an essential practice that parallels source control for application code. Each change to the schema should be captured in a migration script or schema definition file and stored in a versioned repository. This enables teams to track the history of schema modifications, roll back changes if necessary, and synchronize schemas across development, testing, and production environments. Tools such as Flyway, Liquibase, and Alembic provide automated migration frameworks that integrate with continuous integration and deployment pipelines, ensuring that schema changes are applied consistently and in the correct order. These tools also support the concept of idempotency, where migration scripts can be safely re-applied without causing errors, which is particularly useful in dynamic or containerized environments.

Migration planning involves assessing the impact of schema changes, preparing the necessary scripts or tools, coordinating with stakeholders, and validating the results. A typical migration plan begins with a review of the proposed changes, including an analysis of dependencies, risk assessment, and resource requirements. The next step is to prepare migration scripts that perform the necessary alterations, such as altering table definitions, migrating existing data to new structures, and updating indexes or constraints. These scripts must be tested in a staging environment that mirrors production as closely as possible to identify performance regressions, data integrity issues, or unintended side effects.

Data migration, which often accompanies schema changes, presents additional challenges. Moving data from one format or structure to another can be time-consuming, especially for large datasets. Strategies such as online schema changes, lazy migrations, and dual-write mechanisms help minimize disruption. Online schema change tools, like those provided by Percona for MySQL, allow changes to be applied without locking tables or blocking writes. Lazy migration defers the transformation of existing data until it is accessed, distributing the load over time. Dual-write strategies involve writing to both the old and new schemas simultaneously during a transition period, ensuring consistency while allowing for gradual cutover. Each of these strategies must be carefully planned and monitored to avoid data loss or inconsistency.

Schema evolution also requires close coordination with application development teams. Changes to the database schema must be reflected in application code, including data access layers, object-relational mappings, and business logic. Communication between developers and database administrators is essential to ensure that changes are understood, dependencies are identified, and deployment timing is synchronized. In agile development environments, this coordination is often facilitated through sprint planning, integration testing, and shared documentation. Continuous communication helps prevent mismatches between schema and code that can lead to application errors or degraded user experience.

Monitoring and validation are critical during and after schema migrations. Automated tests should verify that data integrity is preserved, queries return correct results, and performance remains within acceptable thresholds. Monitoring tools should track key metrics such as query latency, error rates, and system resource usage to detect any adverse effects of the migration. Post-migration audits can confirm that all changes were applied as intended and that no residual inconsistencies exist in the data. If issues are detected, rollback plans must be in place to revert changes quickly and restore service.

Security and compliance considerations must also be addressed in schema evolution. Changes to data structures may affect access controls, data masking rules, audit logging, or regulatory reporting. For example, adding a column that contains sensitive information requires updating security policies to ensure that only authorized users can access it. Similarly, changes that affect data retention or anonymization processes must be evaluated for compliance with privacy regulations such as GDPR or HIPAA. Governance frameworks should include schema review processes, approval workflows, and documentation standards to ensure that changes align with organizational policies and external requirements.

In distributed and cloud-native architectures, schema evolution becomes even more complex. Databases may span multiple regions, nodes, or containers, each with different latency and consistency characteristics. Schema changes must account for replication delays, eventual consistency models, and failure scenarios. Blue-green deployments, feature flags, and phased rollouts help mitigate risk by allowing changes to be tested incrementally before full deployment. Distributed consensus protocols and schema version negotiation mechanisms may be required in multi-tenant or microservices environments to coordinate schema evolution across independent services.

Schema evolution and migration planning are ongoing activities that reflect the dynamic nature of data and applications. They require a blend of technical precision, process discipline, and cross-functional collaboration. By adopting structured methodologies, leveraging automation tools, and fostering a culture of shared responsibility, organizations can manage schema changes effectively and ensure that their databases remain robust, adaptable, and aligned with business needs. Schema evolution is not merely a technical task but a strategic capability that enables continuous innovation while preserving the stability and integrity of the data ecosystem.

Change Data Capture and Data Lakes

Change Data Capture, commonly known as CDC, is a technique used to identify and track changes made to data in a source system, typically a database, and to propagate those changes to other systems in real time or near real time. Data lakes are large-scale storage repositories that hold raw data in its native format until it is needed for processing or analysis. The integration of CDC with data lakes has become an essential architectural pattern in modern data platforms, particularly in support of real-time analytics, event-driven architectures, and data democratization initiatives. Together, CDC and data lakes address the challenge of ingesting, managing, and analyzing continuously changing data across diverse and distributed environments.

In traditional data processing workflows, data is typically extracted from source systems using batch jobs that run at scheduled intervals. These jobs copy entire tables or datasets, regardless of whether changes have occurred. This approach leads to inefficiencies in storage, processing, and bandwidth consumption. Moreover, it introduces latency, as updates in the source system are not reflected in downstream systems until the next batch run completes. Change Data Capture solves these problems by identifying only the rows that have been inserted, updated, or deleted since the last check and transmitting only those changes. This makes CDC a highly efficient and scalable method for keeping target systems synchronized with minimal overhead.

There are several methods for implementing CDC, each with its own trade-offs in terms of complexity, performance, and system requirements. The most common approaches include database triggers, transaction log reading, and timestamp-based comparisons. Trigger-based CDC uses database triggers to record changes in dedicated audit tables, which are then queried by integration processes. While this method is easy to implement and does not require access to database internals, it can introduce performance penalties due to the overhead of maintaining triggers. Log-based CDC reads the database's transaction log, which records every change as part of its internal recovery mechanism. This approach is highly efficient, non-intrusive, and capable of capturing changes with minimal impact on the source system. Timestamp-based CDC relies on tracking the modification times of records, typically through a last-updated column, and comparing them during each synchronization cycle. This method is simple but can miss changes if timestamps are not accurately maintained or if multiple updates occur between sync intervals.

Data lakes, by design, ingest data from various sources including relational databases, NoSQL stores, application logs, IoT devices, and streaming platforms. The heterogeneous nature of this data and its varying structure, volume, and velocity make data lakes ideal candidates for integration with CDC. As organizations strive to build real-time analytics pipelines, the need to continuously update data lake contents with fresh changes becomes paramount. CDC enables this by serving as the ingestion mechanism that streams updates from operational databases directly into the data lake. This approach ensures that the data lake reflects the current state of business operations, enabling timely and relevant insights across the enterprise.

In practice, implementing CDC in conjunction with data lakes involves the use of data integration platforms, stream processing engines, and cloud-native services. Tools such as Debezium, Apache Kafka, AWS Database Migration Service, and Azure Data Factory offer CDC capabilities that capture changes from various source systems and deliver them to data lake storage such as Amazon S3, Azure Data Lake Storage, or Google Cloud Storage. These changes are often serialized in formats such as Avro, Parquet, or JSON and written to partitioned directories organized by time or data source. Stream processing frameworks like Apache Flink or Apache Spark Structured Streaming can then process this data in motion, transforming, enriching, and routing it to analytical engines or machine learning pipelines.

One of the challenges of using CDC with data lakes is ensuring data consistency and schema evolution management. Because data lakes store raw, often semi-structured data, changes in schema must be carefully tracked and applied to avoid compatibility issues. For example, if a new column is added to a source table, the CDC pipeline must detect and accommodate this change without breaking downstream processing. Schema registries, such as Confluent's Schema Registry for Avro, help manage these changes by versioning schemas and enforcing compatibility checks. Additionally, late-arriving or out-of-order change events can complicate data accuracy, especially in scenarios involving deletions or updates with complex business logic. Implementing idempotent processing, record deduplication, and watermarking strategies can help ensure correctness in such environments.

Security and governance are equally important in CDC-enabled data lake architectures. As sensitive operational data flows into the lake in near real time, access controls, data masking, and encryption must be applied to protect against unauthorized access. Lineage tracking tools are also essential, as they allow organizations to trace data from its origin in the source system through each stage of the CDC pipeline to its final destination in the data lake. This visibility supports regulatory compliance, auditability, and troubleshooting. Metadata management systems that catalog datasets, schema definitions, and update frequencies further enhance the usability and trustworthiness of the data lake.

Performance optimization in CDC for data lakes involves tuning both the capture and delivery mechanisms. Log-based CDC systems must be configured to avoid high latency and backlog accumulation, which can occur during periods of heavy transactional activity. Efficient buffering, batching, and backpressure mechanisms are necessary to handle bursts of changes without overwhelming the pipeline. On the data lake side, write optimization techniques such as compaction, partition pruning, and format conversion reduce storage costs and accelerate query performance. By aligning CDC ingestion with lakehouse paradigms that unify batch and stream processing, organizations can achieve a more flexible and performant data architecture.

CDC and data lakes are not just technical components but strategic enablers of data-driven decision-making. They support real-time dashboards, event-based applications, customer 360 views, and operational intelligence. By enabling continuous data flow from transactional systems into centralized, scalable repositories, CDC makes data lakes more dynamic, current, and actionable. Organizations that implement robust CDC pipelines into their data lake architectures gain a significant advantage in agility, responsiveness, and analytical capability. The integration of these technologies marks a shift from static data processing toward a real-time, responsive, and unified data ecosystem that mirrors the pace and complexity of modern digital enterprises.

Observability and Logging Best Practices

Observability and logging best practices form the backbone of reliable, maintainable, and secure data infrastructure. In modern database systems and data-driven applications, the ability to understand what is happening within the system at any given time is crucial for detecting anomalies, diagnosing issues, ensuring uptime, and optimizing performance. Observability is more than monitoring. It is the capacity to infer internal states of the system based on its external outputs. This includes logs, metrics, and traces, which together provide a comprehensive view of system behavior. Logging, specifically, plays a central role by recording discrete events and contextual data that can be analyzed later to explain or predict system activity. When implemented with discipline and intention, observability and logging empower teams to manage complexity and achieve high availability with confidence.

A foundational principle in observability is to treat logs, metrics, and traces not as optional features but as essential components of the system. This requires embedding instrumentation from the earliest design phases and integrating it deeply into the software architecture. Logs are especially important because they provide human-readable accounts of system events, errors, warnings, and informational messages. Each log entry should contain a timestamp, a severity level, the component or module producing the log, and a clear, structured message. Adding contextual metadata such as user identifiers, request IDs, session tokens, and database transaction IDs allows logs to be correlated across services, making it easier to trace the flow of requests and identify root causes of failures.

Structured logging is a best practice that enhances the usability of logs. Instead of emitting plain text messages, applications should produce logs in a structured format such as JSON. Structured logs enable machine parsing, indexing, and querying in centralized logging platforms. They also facilitate automated alerting, dashboard generation, and anomaly detection. By making logs more consistent and searchable, structured logging improves visibility and supports faster troubleshooting. However, structured logging requires discipline in defining log schemas, choosing meaningful field names, and avoiding overly verbose or redundant messages.

Another key aspect of effective logging is log level management. Logging systems typically support multiple severity levels, including DEBUG, INFO, WARN, ERROR, and FATAL. Choosing the appropriate level for each message is essential to avoid log noise and ensure that important information is not drowned out. DEBUG logs are useful during development and for diagnosing complex issues but should be disabled or filtered in production to reduce storage overhead. INFO logs provide general visibility into system behavior and are often retained in production environments. WARN and ERROR logs signal potential and actual problems, respectively, and should trigger alerts or reviews. FATAL logs indicate critical failures that require immediate intervention. Maintaining clear policies around log levels helps teams balance verbosity and relevance.

Centralized log aggregation is another best practice that simplifies management and enhances observability. In distributed systems, logs are produced by multiple services running across various nodes, containers, or geographic regions. Collecting all logs into a central repository allows unified search, analysis, and correlation. Tools like Elasticsearch, Logstash, Kibana (the ELK stack), Fluentd, Splunk, and Loki provide powerful platforms for indexing, visualizing, and managing large volumes of log data. Centralized logging also supports retention policies, access control, and compliance auditing, which are essential for maintaining security and meeting regulatory requirements.

Security and privacy considerations must be integrated into logging practices from the start. Logs can inadvertently expose sensitive data if not properly sanitized. This includes passwords, encryption keys, personal identifiers, financial information, or confidential business logic. Developers must ensure that sensitive fields are masked, redacted, or excluded entirely from logs. Additionally, access to logs should be restricted based on role and necessity, and log data should be encrypted both in transit and at rest. Audit logs, which track administrative actions and user access to data, require special handling to ensure integrity and non-repudiation. These logs must be immutable and stored in tamper-evident formats to support forensic analysis and regulatory compliance.

Correlating logs with metrics and traces enhances the depth of observability. Metrics provide quantitative measures of system health, such as query latency, memory usage, connection counts, and error rates. Traces capture the flow of a request through multiple services, including timing and execution paths. When logs include identifiers that match those in traces and metrics, it becomes possible to build rich, contextual narratives about what happened, why it happened, and how to fix it. This correlation supports proactive monitoring, root cause analysis, and performance tuning. Platforms like OpenTelemetry, Prometheus, and Jaeger offer integrated frameworks for collecting and correlating observability data across diverse systems.

Observability also extends to log retention and lifecycle management. Not all logs need to be stored indefinitely, and excessive retention can lead to compliance issues, storage costs, and operational overhead. Organizations must define retention policies that align with business needs, regulatory requirements, and incident investigation timelines. Critical logs, such as security audits or transactional records, may need to be preserved for years, while DEBUG logs may be discarded within hours. Automated tools should enforce these policies, rotating logs regularly, archiving older data, and purging expired entries. Retention strategies should also consider the format and granularity of logs, ensuring that essential insights are retained while unnecessary noise is minimized.

Testing and validation are important to ensure that observability mechanisms are functioning as intended. Logging should be included in test plans, with automated checks to verify that expected events are logged correctly under various conditions. During incident simulations or chaos engineering exercises, the quality and usefulness of logs should be evaluated. Can the logs answer key questions? Do they reveal bottlenecks or failure points? Are they easy to interpret under pressure? These exercises help refine logging practices and build trust in the observability infrastructure.

Team culture plays a significant role in the effectiveness of observability. Engineers must understand the value of good logging and be encouraged to write informative, structured logs as part of their development workflow. Code reviews should include evaluation of logging practices, and observability should be a first-class consideration in system design. Observability maturity can be measured not only by the tools in place but by how deeply observability is embedded into the development, deployment, and operations lifecycle. Teams that prioritize observability are better equipped to deliver reliable systems, respond to incidents quickly, and iterate with confidence.

In dynamic and complex environments, where microservices, containers, and serverless functions interact at scale, observability and logging are indispensable. They provide the transparency needed to manage change, ensure performance, and deliver value to users. Through structured logging, centralized aggregation, secure handling, and thoughtful retention, organizations can build observability systems that support continuous learning, rapid recovery, and sustained operational excellence. As systems continue to grow in complexity, the ability to observe, understand, and act on what is happening within them will remain one of the most critical capabilities of modern data architecture.

Continuous Integration for Database Code

Continuous integration for database code is a critical practice in modern software development that ensures database changes are developed, tested, and delivered in a reliable and automated fashion. As applications evolve rapidly and deployment cycles become shorter, it becomes essential for database development to keep pace with application code. This means treating database schema, stored procedures, triggers, seed data, and even database configuration as code, subject to the same principles of version control, automated testing, and validation. The goal is to enable teams to deliver database changes with the same confidence and agility as application code, avoiding the risks traditionally associated with manual updates, inconsistent environments, and fragile deployments.

The foundation of continuous integration for database code lies in version control. All database artifacts should be stored in a version-controlled repository alongside application code. This includes schema definitions, migration scripts, DDL statements, seed data files, and test scripts. By managing database code in version control, teams gain visibility into change history, facilitate collaboration, and ensure that changes can be reviewed, audited, and reverted if necessary. Branching strategies, such as trunk-based development or feature branches, can be applied to database code just as they are with application logic, allowing isolated development and safe integration of new features.

Once database code is under version control, the next step is to automate its validation. Every change to the database code should trigger a pipeline that validates the correctness and compatibility of the changes. This includes linting SQL syntax, running static analysis to detect anti-patterns, and applying the changes to a temporary database instance to verify their behavior. Automated database builds are essential for catching errors early and ensuring that changes do not break the existing structure or introduce regressions. Tools such as Flyway, Liquibase, DbUp, and Redgate SQL Change Automation allow developers to define database changes as scripts or migrations and to apply them in a controlled and repeatable manner.

Testing is a central component of continuous integration for databases. Just as unit tests verify the correctness of application logic, database tests validate that schema changes behave as expected, stored procedures produce correct results, and data transformations maintain integrity. These tests should be run automatically as part of the integration pipeline, using a fresh database instance created from scratch or restored from a baseline snapshot. Test data should be seeded deterministically, and test cases should cover both positive and negative scenarios. Tests must be isolated, reproducible, and fast to execute, supporting rapid feedback and enabling developers to iterate quickly. Database testing frameworks such as tSQLt, utPLSQL, and DBUnit provide mechanisms for organizing and executing tests within the database context.

An often overlooked but vital aspect of continuous integration for database code is the management of migration scripts. Unlike application binaries, which can be overwritten, databases are stateful systems that retain historical data. Changes must therefore be applied incrementally and in the correct sequence. Migration scripts must be idempotent where possible or clearly versioned and ordered to avoid conflicts and ensure deterministic results. Each script should include both the forward change and the rollback logic to support recovery in case of errors. These scripts should be executed in a controlled environment during the CI pipeline to ensure they apply cleanly and result in the expected schema state.

Integration pipelines for database code must also include environment validation. Since databases often behave differently depending on configuration, hardware, or data volume, CI pipelines should replicate production conditions as closely as possible. Containerization using Docker is a powerful technique for achieving this consistency. By defining database images with specific configurations and dependencies, teams can ensure that every developer, tester, and pipeline runs against the same environment. Containers also make it easier to spin up isolated environments for parallel testing and reduce dependency on shared infrastructure. Kubernetes and orchestration tools can manage these containers at scale, supporting high-availability test clusters and ephemeral test databases.

Continuous integration practices must extend beyond the technical mechanics to include collaboration, documentation, and review. Code reviews for database changes are as important as those for application code. Changes should be peer-reviewed to catch errors, enforce standards, and share knowledge across the team. Schema changes should be documented clearly, with explanations of their purpose, impact, and rollback plans. Documentation should also describe dependencies between schema elements and application logic, highlighting areas that require coordinated releases or phased rollouts. When schema changes are complex or risky, feature toggles, blue-green deployments, or canary migrations can be employed to reduce impact and ensure a smooth transition.

Security considerations are integral to continuous integration for databases. Pipelines must enforce access controls to ensure that only authorized users can make schema changes, especially in shared or production-like environments. Secrets such as database credentials must be stored securely using vaults or environment variables, not hardcoded into scripts or configuration files. Static analysis tools should scan database code for security vulnerabilities such as SQL injection, improper permissions, or unencrypted sensitive data. Compliance requirements such as GDPR, HIPAA, or PCI DSS may also dictate specific rules around data retention, anonymization, and audit logging, which must be enforced and tested during the CI process.

Monitoring and observability should be built into the CI pipeline to track the success and performance of database operations. Metrics such as migration duration, test pass rates, and schema drift incidents provide insight into the health of the database lifecycle. Logging mechanisms should capture detailed output from migration scripts, test executions, and validation checks, making it easy to trace failures and debug issues. Alerts and dashboards can notify teams when pipeline steps fail or when performance thresholds are breached, enabling proactive response and continuous improvement.

Ultimately, continuous integration for database code transforms database development from a manual, error-prone process into a structured, automated, and collaborative discipline. It bridges the historical divide between developers and database administrators by introducing shared tools, practices, and goals. By automating validation, testing, and deployment, CI reduces the risk of production incidents, accelerates delivery timelines, and increases confidence in the reliability of changes. When properly implemented, continuous integration becomes a powerful enabler of agile development, allowing organizations to innovate quickly while maintaining the stability and integrity of their most valuable asset: their data.

Future Trends in Database Optimization and Backup

The future of database optimization and backup is being reshaped by the evolving demands of modern applications, the explosive growth of data, and the increasing complexity of hybrid and cloud-native architectures. Organizations today require databases that can adapt to changing workloads in real time, minimize downtime, ensure data integrity, and support analytics at scale. As a result, optimization and backup strategies are undergoing a fundamental transformation, driven by advances in automation, artificial intelligence, distributed systems, and new storage paradigms. These trends are not just incremental improvements but represent a shift in how databases are managed, safeguarded, and optimized for performance and resilience.

One of the most prominent trends in database optimization is the increased reliance on autonomous systems powered by artificial intelligence and machine learning. Autonomous databases can automatically tune performance parameters, choose the best indexes, balance workloads, and allocate resources without human intervention. These systems learn from query patterns, system metrics, and historical performance data to make real-time adjustments. By analyzing workload characteristics, autonomous optimization engines can predict query performance, identify bottlenecks, and proactively apply optimizations such as index creation, SQL rewrites, and memory allocation changes. This shift reduces the need for manual performance tuning, democratizes access to database optimization expertise, and enables faster adaptation to fluctuating workloads.

Cloud-native and multi-cloud architectures are also influencing the direction of database optimization and backup strategies. With the rise of containerized applications, serverless computing, and microservices, databases must scale elastically and operate reliably across distributed environments. Future optimization efforts will focus on dynamic workload distribution, where queries and transactions are intelligently routed to the most optimal nodes or regions based on real-time load, latency, and cost considerations. This requires the integration of distributed query planners, global indexing strategies, and adaptive data sharding mechanisms that can re-balance data automatically as usage patterns shift. Backup systems will also need to evolve to support consistent and rapid recovery in multi-region and multi-cloud scenarios, ensuring that critical data remains protected regardless of where it resides.

Another major development is the growing adoption of real-time and continuous optimization techniques. Traditional optimization often occurs periodically through scheduled maintenance tasks such as index rebuilding, statistics updates, or defragmentation. However, future systems will increasingly perform these tasks continuously in the background without interrupting user workloads. This is made possible through advancements in background processing, non-blocking algorithms, and fine-grained locking mechanisms. Similarly, backup systems are transitioning from full and incremental snapshots taken at intervals to continuous data protection models that capture every change in real time. These change streams can be used to reconstruct the state of the database at any point in time, supporting instant recovery, point-in-time restores, and forensic analysis.

Data tiering and intelligent storage optimization are also gaining traction as data volumes grow beyond the limits of traditional infrastructure. Modern databases are expected to support tiered storage architectures, where hot, warm, and cold data are stored on different media based on access frequency and performance requirements. Future optimization engines will incorporate data access pattern analysis to automatically classify and move data between storage tiers, reducing costs while maintaining performance for active datasets. Backup systems will leverage similar intelligence to prioritize critical data, compress rarely accessed information, and offload archival content to low-cost, long-retention cloud storage services. Integration with object storage, immutable storage, and storage-level snapshots will become standard features of enterprise-grade backup solutions.

Security and compliance requirements are also driving innovation in database optimization and backup. As regulations become stricter and data privacy expectations increase, future systems will embed security-aware optimization features that enforce encryption, data masking, and access control policies during optimization and backup processes. Query optimizers will be designed to minimize exposure of sensitive data, and backup systems will be required to support encryption at rest and in transit, secure key management, and audit logging. Zero trust architectures and secure enclaves may become part of the optimization pipeline, ensuring that no unprotected data ever leaves a secure boundary during maintenance or backup operations.

Edge computing is another trend influencing future database technologies. As more data is generated and processed at the edge, databases must support decentralized optimization and backup strategies. Lightweight, embedded database engines will perform local optimizations based on limited resources, while synchronizing periodically with centralized systems. Backup strategies at the edge will need to account for limited connectivity, using techniques such as forward error correction, opportunistic replication, and delta encoding to ensure data durability and availability even in constrained environments. These edge-capable systems must also maintain consistency across distributed nodes and support seamless failover and recovery when failures occur.

Observability and proactive diagnostics will also play a larger role in future database optimization. Enhanced telemetry will enable granular visibility into query execution paths, resource consumption, and contention points. This data will feed into machine learning models that provide predictive diagnostics and automated remediation recommendations. As observability tools become more tightly integrated with database engines, administrators will gain real-time insights into optimization opportunities and backup health status. Metrics such as backup success rates, recovery point objectives, and mean time to restore will be continuously monitored and visualized in dashboards that support decision-making and compliance reporting.

The shift toward database-as-a-service models also influences optimization and backup trends. As more organizations adopt managed database platforms, the responsibility for optimization and backup shifts to the service provider. This allows businesses to focus on application development while relying on the provider's expertise and infrastructure to ensure database health and availability. In these environments, optimization and backup operations must be transparent, auditable, and customizable to meet diverse application needs. Service-level objectives will dictate the frequency, granularity, and retention of backups, as well as the latency and consistency of optimization efforts.

As artificial intelligence becomes more sophisticated, predictive analytics will further enhance database optimization. Future systems will not only react to existing performance issues but also anticipate them. By modeling query trends, data growth patterns, and resource utilization trajectories, AI-driven engines will forecast when indexes will become ineffective, when storage will be saturated, or when backups will exceed time windows. This foresight will enable proactive scaling, reconfiguration, and data pruning, reducing the likelihood of performance degradation or backup failures during critical operations.

Overall, the future of database optimization and backup is defined by intelligence, automation, and adaptability. These systems will become more self-aware, more integrated with broader IT ecosystems, and more responsive to business demands. By embracing continuous learning, real-time processing, and distributed architecture principles, the next generation of database technologies will empower organizations to manage data with unprecedented precision, reliability, and speed. The convergence of optimization and backup as integral components of a unified data management strategy ensures that databases will remain not just passive repositories of information, but dynamic engines of operational and analytical power in the years to come.

www.ingramcontent.com/pod-product-compliance
Lightning Source LLC
La Vergne TN
LVHW051236050326
832903LV00028B/2433